Give
Voice
To What Unites Us

By Sheri Rosen

Renewing employee communication excellence through intentional purpose, delivery and conversation

International Association
of Business Communicators

**International Association
of Business Communicators**

155 Montgomery St. Suite 1210
San Francisco, CA 94104

ABOUT THE AUTHOR

Employee communication and technology enthusiast—that is how Sheri Rosen describes herself on LinkedIn. Sheri has led companies to communication success in the banking and financial services, health care, and energy industries; for nonprofit associations; and as a consultant. She has won international recognition for thought leadership and communication skills and is a highly rated seminar speaker. Sheri is an Accredited Business Communicator and a Fellow of the International Association of Business Communicators.

TABLE OF CONTENTS

INTRODUCTION

Time brings wisdom, appreciation of achievement and a certain expectation of continuing accomplishments. It can also dampen enthusiasm, slow movement and blur vision. Just ask my mother. When she recently went to renew her driver's license, she failed the vision test. She hadn't realized she wasn't seeing clearly, but it makes sense in retrospect. She'd been feeling unsteady as she walked, and it was no wonder. Her vision in each eye was different. She literally was seeing unlevel ground because the spatial feedback from each side of her brain didn't balance.

Employee communication—connecting people for company success—as a business discipline is maturing, too. Over the years, employee communication has lost its balance in some companies, and without it, work can literally slow down and lose focus. In vibrant companies, on the other hand, people progress in sync by talking through workplace matters. Conversation is essential to business, but it is often rushed and underappreciated in the strain and structure of the corporate world.

A pair of eyeglasses gave my mother "new" eyes. And that is what this book can do for you—let you see employee communication with a new focus. If you have been an employee communication director for a while, you know how completely different the landscape looks now than it did 10—or even just five—years ago. Still, you bring relevant perspective, wisdom and an appreciation for how the business works. If you are young and brand new to the field, you bring a fresh filter to employee communication. The post-9/11 world, economic uncertainty, global business and social media are normal to you. Both communication wisdom and a fresh point of view can elevate excellent communication amid the pressures and politics of the business world.

I come at this from the perspective of studying and practicing employee communication in small and large organizations, living and working around the globe, leading online communities and social media, and experiencing layoffs. I stopped to ask, where is the uncharted territory, the future for this discipline?

Where is the uncharted territory, the future for this discipline?

This book is the result of that question. How can we be excellent at employee communication, today, in whatever job or circumstance we find ourselves? This book will rearrange how you see your respective pieces of this jigsaw puzzle of experiences and expectations to fit them all together as a coherent, complete picture. In short, it tells the story of excellent employee communication.[1]

INSIGHT NO. 1: COMMUNICATE TO THRIVE

One truth, consistent for organizations of all sizes and in all industries, is that companies thrive and survive when employees have two things:[2]

1. Supportive relationships on the job
2. Information about how their work furthers business goals

This book examines how these two fundamentals and their associated puzzle pieces interlock on the employee communication planning table. Just as if we were starting a jigsaw puzzle, we will arrange related pieces as we spread them out on the table. You may require a bigger (or smaller) table than the one you start with, or you may need to pull up a chair for someone else to help, someone you didn't anticipate would be able to offer useful guidance. You may be used to borrowing ideas from companies in the same industry, with a similar geographical scope, or with comparable competitive challenges or business needs. Let's look further.

INSIGHT NO. 2: COMMUNICATE WITH STRENGTH

This book will enable you to identify relevant patterns of excellence in communication from dissimilar companies—specifically, ones of a different size from your own. We'll examine how employee communication excellence in large companies is not typically the same as excellence in micro or mid-sized companies. However—and this is a major point—distinct communication strengths can transcend size. In fact, there are instances when big companies should communicate like small ones, and vice versa. There are specific ways to do this, especially within the ever-growing sphere of social media.

How? Deliver information in a way that people can understand, through the following:

1. Conversation

2. Operational processes

3. Media

INSIGHT NO. 3: COMMUNICATE FOR PEOPLE

Employee communication excellence is not about the most elaborate plan or the latest technology. It's about people, who devote the largest chunk of their waking hours to their jobs. They deserve our best. This book will look at specific ways to transcend company size using the strengths and opportunities of conversation, operational processes and media in companies of all sizes. What these organizations have in common is a willingness to:

1. Improve understanding through dialogue with an *intentional purpose*.

2. Engage in complex and sometimes job-changing discussions that are *intentionally delivered*.

3. Unite employees through *intentional conversations* in ways that can be personally relevant.

That's not only excellent communication; it's excellent management.

Notes

1 Copyrighted charts in this book are licensed under Creative Commons, allowing you to use, share and build upon them as long as you give attribution to the author. Keep the conversation going; visit http://creativecommons.org/licenses/by-sa/3.0/

2 For an example of the link between excellent employee communication and corporate financial success: Towers Watson. (2009). Capitalizing on effective communication: How courage, innovation and discipline drive business results in challenging times. Retrieved from http://www.towerswatson.com/en/Insights/IC-Types/Survey-Research-Results/2009/12/20092010-Communication-ROI-Study-Report-Capitalizing-on-Effective-Communication

CHAPTER 1: ACHIEVE EXCELLENT COMMUNICATION

"If you want to achieve excellence, you can get there today. As of this second, quit doing less-than-excellent work."—Thomas J. Watson Sr.

Watson spoke with credibility. In the earliest days of computing, he presided over IBM's rise to dominance and inspired its corporate culture of loyalty.

How can you achieve excellence in employee communication and leave behind your less-than-excellent work, starting today?

Communication specialists in small companies might be rolling their eyes at this point, frustrated that they don't have the budget or staff to produce award-winning communication programs like their large-company counterparts. In contrast, corporate communication directors who have the funds for attractive, appealing media and highly skilled staff have different barriers to excellent employee communication. Anything resembling the best communication gets shredded as it is pushed through the bureaucracy of approvals.

Of course, it all depends on how you define excellence. James Grunig led a research team to study what makes corporate communication excellent in the highly influential *Excellence* study (which includes the books *Excellence in Public Relations and Communication Management, Excellent Public Relations and Effective Organizations,* and *Manager's Guide to Excellence in Public Relations and Communication Management*).

The answer—your route to excellence—is a twist on the two-way communication model with a sender and receiver.

> What gets in the way of achieving excellent communication in your organization?
> - Time
> - Money
> - Staff size
> - Approval process
> - Management support
> - Skills
> - Experience
> - Authority
> - Knowledge
>
> Perhaps it's not what you think.

The traditional, simple, two-way communication model does not automatically lead to excellent communication

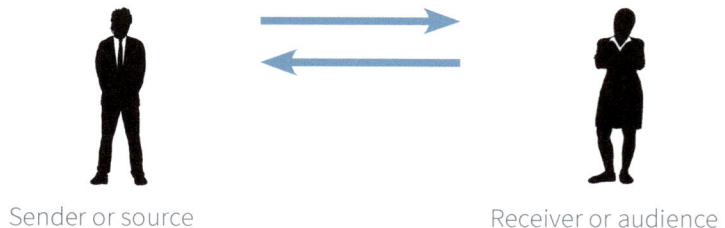

Sender or source

Receiver or audience

Complete communication requires more than sending a message; someone has to receive it and acknowledge it. Beaming signals into the sky on the off chance that light years from now intergalactic aliens will see them is similar to hoping employees will notice when someone broadcasts a message they don't care about or understand. Two-way communication requires an exchange, a response; feedback closes the loop. The sender knows the receiver got the message and whether it made sense.

To represent excellent communication, this simple model needs more. The topic and the outcome of the exchange are what offer the next twist, according to the Grunig research, using two distinct variations on the two-way communication model.[1]

That's right. There are two types of two-way communication: asymmetrical and symmetrical. Excellence is reflected not in asymmetrical communication, which is off balance or unequal. Instead, excellence is achieved with balanced, symmetrical communication.

Asymmetrical	Symmetrical
Two-way communication between the sender [organization] and receiver [employees] in which the sender uses research about the receiver to create messages that will persuade the receiver to behave as the sender wants.	Two-way communication between the sender [organization] and receiver [employees] in which the sender uses communication to manage confict and improve understanding through dialogue with the receiver.

Seen side by side, the two definitions start off similarly, with communication as a two-way proposition. They diverge, however, in their reason for two-way communication:

- Asymmetrical communication is used for persuasion—to drive business goals, for example. Based on factors the receiver reveals in feedback, the sender figures out how to create more persuasive messages as the exchange continues.

Asymmetrical communication

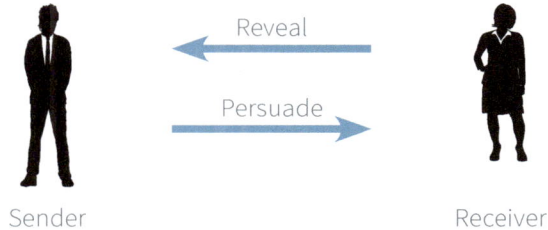

Reveal

Persuade

Sender   Receiver

- Symmetrical communication is used for clarity and confirmation—for example, to clarify a business goal and confirm what support an employee will need to achieve it. Symmetrical communication is an ongoing dialogue, a continual loop, to provide clarity and manage conflict as a step toward shared understanding.

Symmetrical communication

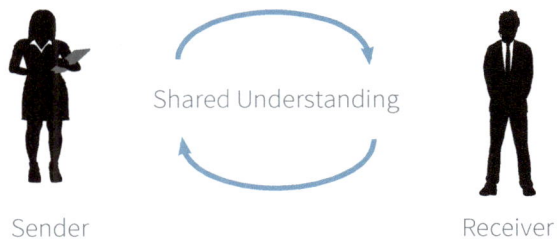

Shared Understanding

Sender   Receiver

The word "conflict" as used here doesn't mean physical or emotional battles, but it does represent the misunderstandings or lack of agreement that exists in every workplace. Reaching a common or shared meaning requires truly listening to each other. Asymmetrical communication may include a two-way exchange of information, such as giving and acknowledging a directive, but the receiver isn't expected to have questions and the sender isn't open to suggestions. Taking time to understand the other person's thoughts on a subject, and perhaps changing your mind as a result, is what distinguishes symmetrical communication from asymmetrical communication.

"You can't just charge in saying, 'You're wrong, and I'm right,'" Jonathan Haidt said in his TED Talk video, which has been viewed more than a million times. He opined that our human history of cooperation among groups—people pursuing higher ends—is the greatest wonder of the world. "Everybody thinks they are right. A lot of the problems we have to solve are problems that require us to change other people. And if you want to change other people, a much better way to do it is to first understand who we are."[2]

For people to cooperate in companies, to solve problems and to succeed, they need symmetrical communication. With excellent employee communication, employees and the organization will get closer to a common understanding of what matters and what they hope for in their work.

MANAGEMENT BIAS AND MORALE

The notion of employee communication excellence has taken shape as the business world has evolved over the past 100 years. For a while, industrial managers experimented with techniques to persuade workers to produce more. The Hawthorne effect[3] is a term coined to describe the results of factory experiments in the 1920s and 1930s that ultimately revealed extra lighting or cleaner workspaces did not increase productivity. Instead, the extra attention management paid to the workers involved in the productivity experiment was what motivated them. This finding led to the conclusion that the right information could persuade employees to act to the benefit of the company, and therefore, communication was seen as a way to influence employees to be more efficient and productive. That is practically a definition of asymmetrical communication—the opposite of excellence.

> **Employee communication vs. internal communications**
>
> *Lawyer vs. barrister*
> *Doctor vs. physician*
>
> While "internal communications" may be the more common phrase in Europe and Asia, "employee communication" seems to be a North American preference. My choice for this book is "employee communication" for two reasons:
>
> - "Employee" keeps the focus on people; "internal" implies a place.
> - Communication implies an ongoing pattern of conversation; communications, with an "s," implies tools or documents.

To keep employees happy and productive, and to make companies successful, researchers in the last century also studied how information flows through an organization—or becomes distorted along the way. They studied whether communication appears adequate or credible to employees. Researchers focused on channels and methods for communicating, particularly between employees and their supervisors. This research offered evidence that effective communication equated to employee satisfaction. Open and complete communication from top management, rather than the amount of communication, affected morale. Specifically, employees wanted top management to explain company operations.[4]

Theorists concluded that without communication, there could be no motivation, no leadership, no productivity and ultimately no organization.[5]

While that assessment may seem to justify budgeting resources for employee communication, it misses the point of excellent symmetrical communication, which involves people talking and listening to each other to reach a shared understanding.

Grunig turned accepted wisdom on its head: "Such variables as motivation, leadership and productivity affect the way people communicate in an organization."[6]

Is it a chicken or egg conundrum? No.

Excellent management comes first so that excellent employee communication can be integrated into daily operations.

Excellent management comes first so that excellent employee communication can be integrated into daily operations.

Furthermore, excellent management is willing to enter into often-messy conversations with employees about complex and life-changing workplace issues.

Furthermore, excellent management is willing to enter into often-messy conversations with employees about complex and life-changing workplace issues.

Who exactly will have these complex and messy conversations with employees as they work? Not the "undercover boss" of the reality television series. Each episode features a different CEO who disguises himself (and it is usually a he) in order to join front-line employees and hear their thoughts about work and life. As *Time* magazine opined, it can be "a manipulative, cheesy piece of big-network PR for executives looking to burnish their image."[7] Becoming one of the guys doesn't solve problems in our current age of transparency, not to mention that it is a one-shot effort. While *Undercover Boss* may reveal a specific problem or process to fix, integrating employee communication into daily operations is entirely different, and few CEOs come out of an episode with a plan for ongoing, symmetrical communication.

WHO, THEN?

So if the answer isn't to have the CEO transform into an in-the-trenches employee, who should take responsibility for ongoing symmetrical communication? Who should participate in the dialogue or at least moderate it?

The *Excellence* study insists it be a professional communication specialist.

But what happens if, as is the case in many small companies, there isn't an employee communication specialist?

Here is what we know so far:

- Communication as persuasion is limiting.
- Communication without excellent management struggles to create motivation, productivity or leadership.
- Communication that helps individuals reach a shared understanding is the definition of excellence.
- Communication excels in organizations where motivation, productivity and leadership set the stage for dialogue among all of us—toward shared meaning.

Here is what we still need to learn:

- Who is responsible for excellent communication?
- How do we build excellence into communication?

Notes

1   Grunig, J. E. (1992). *Excellence in public relations and communication management*. Hillsdale, New Jersey: L. Erlbaum Associates, p. 18.

2   Haidt, J. (2008, Sept). Jonathan Haidt: The moral roots of liberals and conservatives [video]. Retrieved from http://www.ted.com/talks/lang/en/jonathan_haidt_on_the_moral_mind.html

3   Harvard professor Elton Mayo conducted productivity and morale experiments at the Hawthorne Works division of Western Electric in suburban Chicago in the 1920s and 1930s. He manipulated physical and environmental factors in the workplace as well as psychological aspects. The results of these studies changed accepted theory. The best-known result, called the Hawthorne effect, showed that simply because individuals were singled out for study, their behavior changed. Overall, the study showed that formal and informal relationships among employees and their supervisors had an effect on behavior and motivation. The Hawthorne effect has been written about in many places, including:
Hawthorne effect. (n.d.). Retrieved October 1, 2011, from Wikipedia: http://en.wikipedia.org/wiki/Hawthorne_effect

4   Early researchers looked at how information flows through an organization and affects morale and satisfaction:
Roethlisberger, F. J., Dickson, W. J., Wright, H. A., & Pforzheimer, C. H. (1939). *Management and the worker: An account of a research program conducted by the Western Electric Company, Hawthorne Works, Chicago*. Cambridge, Massachusetts: Harvard University Press.

Redding, W. D. (1985). Stumbling toward identity: The emergence of organizational communication as a field of study. In R. D. McPhee & P. K. Tompkins (Eds.) *Organizational communication: Traditional themes and new directions* (pp. 15–54). Newbury Park, CA: SAGE Publications.

Putnam, L., & Cheny, G. (1985). Organizational communication: Historical development and future directions. In F. M. Jablin, L. L. Putnam, K. H. Roberts & L. W. Porter (Eds.) *Handbook of organizational communication: An interdisciplinary perspective* (pp. 549–599). Newbury Park, CA: SAGE Publications.

5   Grunig attributes the thought that without communication there can be no motivation, no leadership, no productivity, and no organization to:
Goldhaber, G. M. (1984). *Information strategies: New pathways to management productivity* (Rev. ed.). Norwood, NJ: Ablex Pub. Corp., quoted in Grunig, ibid, p. 548.

6   And then, Grunig turns that thought on its head:
Grunig, J. E. (1992). *Excellence in public relations and communication management*. Hillsdale, New Jersey: L. Erlbaum Associates, p. 548.

7   Poniewozik, J. (February 8, 2010). *Undercover Boss* Is Phony and Manipulative. But Don't Hold That Against It [blog]. Retrieved from http://entertainment.time.com/2010/02/08/undercover-boss-bless-its-phony-manipulative-heart/

CHAPTER 2: DROP THE ASSUMPTION THAT IT WON'T WORK HERE

My son, who is in college, recently struggled with a writing assignment unlike any he had faced before. It was an intertwined topic, both vague and complex. He needed to understand the big-picture concept and then write engagingly about the details. He couldn't quite envision how to structure the paper to match the goal of the assignment—and please the professor. And, of course, there was a looming deadline.

He first had to clear the clutter in his mind to make space for new thoughts, so he rearranged his bedroom furniture and recategorized his collection of CDs and classic LPs. Clear the clutter, clear the mind. Next, he tried diving deeply into the assignment with a quieted and open mind. And it worked, because he now had the mental energy to be open to new thoughts.

BREAK EXISTING PATTERNS

One thing my son didn't do was copy from someone else, even in a world where just about everything you can think of is a Google search away. He had to come up with an innovative idea and implement it with exactitude. He struggled, like we do, to recognize that originality may simply be a different view of something familiar. Creativity is the ability to break out of our existing way of thinking and see patterns in a new way.[1] Sometimes we discover familiar patterns in unexpected places that we can rearrange to solve our assignment.

> ## Originality may simply be a different view of something familiar.

We can't easily take another company's successful communication program and drop it into our organization, even if imitation is flattery and Google makes it easy to find. Merely copying someone else doesn't solve our particular quandary. Experienced employee communication directors know their companies have unique cultures, histories, expectations and operating styles. This doesn't stop us from scouring the Internet, buying books and attending conferences to learn how others have achieved communication success, only to conclude we could never do it like that at our company because the boss wouldn't consider it, we don't have the money for that kind of campaign or we presume another obstacle, real or perceived. It's easy to assume our communication challenges are unlike those anyone else has faced. We need to generate creative ideas to solve problems specific to our respective companies.

We pick up pieces of knowledge during this scavenger hunt and end up with many nuggets and ideas we hope will be useful someday. But what can we apply in an original, useful way?

Let's clear our minds and dive into different patterns of thinking about employee communication. You won't necessarily come up with a campaign to copy, but you will understand *why* it worked in another place so you can assess whether it could improve your own communication plan.

Our assignment: Create communication that helps individuals reach a shared understanding, the definition of excellent communication.

Our objective: Engage employees to reach goals.

As study after study shows, companies thrive when employees feel connected to their work.[2] To feel this connection and to achieve business success, employees need two things:

1. Supportive relationships on the job
2. Information about how their work fits in and furthers business goals

The CEO of Insync Surveys, James Garriock, said of his firm's 2011 survey of workers in Australia and New Zealand: "Employees want to know their work is meaningful and connected to the organisation's goals. Strong communication creates this link because people feel respected and empowered if they're informed about things that matter to them."[3]

We often look to other companies within our industry for ideas about how to connect employees to the business. We also look to other companies of similar size. As a way of recategorizing the puzzle pieces of communication, in this book we will purposely look at companies that seem completely different—especially ones of a different size.

That's because the answer to the question in Chapter 1, "Who is responsible for symmetrical communication?" depends to a large degree on the size of the company. Companies of different sizes traditionally excel in different methods of employee communication. By breaking out of presumed constraints (like company size), we can rearrange the pieces to address the goals of any communication assignment.

ORGANIZE THE CLUTTER

Thinking about all the possible ways of creating and delivering communication that engages employees can be overwhelming. We need a way to organize and categorize the options so we can more easily decide who will take responsibility for symmetrical communication.

Let's clear the clutter in our minds. Imagine that you are in a library sorting books, first by their color, then shape, and finally popularity. Now, instead, visualize those books as artifacts that tell your company's story. Sort the volumes you've chosen to keep, rather than hand off to the used bookstore, in a bookcase designated for business goals and corporate culture. What do the books look like? Which subjects or well-worn stories keep everyone reading? Companies of different sizes would fill these shelves in particular ways, precisely because of the organization's size. From bookcase to bookcase, company to company, the

---

I feel supported when:

- Someone listens to me in a way that makes me feel respected.
- Someone values my contributions.
- Someone cares for my well-being.

When I feel supported, I am likely to help other employees and customers.

Small enough for whom?

Researchers have to define small in order to determine which businesses to survey. Should the factor be annual revenue? Market dominance? Geographic scope of operation? Not surprisingly, the defining factor for studying employee communication excellence turns out to be the number of employees. Workforce size affects communication practices.

When does a business qualify as small? Both U.S. and Canadian officials put a break point at fewer than 500 employees, and that is the demarcation used in this book, though Europeans are more likely to delineate firms with 250 employees or fewer as small.

The U.S. Small Business Administration reported that the small-business atmosphere is one of rapid change and a sense of impermanence. Not very different from large businesses nowadays.

various communication methods on display and their content make patterns, not alphabetically or by industry or geography, but by company size. The shelves for small businesses—both micro and mid-sized companies—include artifacts of different styles of communication than the ones found on shelves for large businesses. Looking at the artifacts this way, we can see how employee communication strengths form patterns in different-sized companies.

The patterns look like this:

Company size	Employee communication strength
Micro-business (up to 20 employees)	CEO as communicator through conversation about business goals and culture
Mid-sized business (21 to 500 employees)	Communication of goals and culture integrated within business operations and processes
Large business (more than 500 employees)	Consistent messages through internal "mass" media to improve understanding of strategic goals and culture

What exactly does this chart tell us?

In very small companies, called micro-businesses, supportive interactions and strategic information-sharing occur naturally through conversations and storytelling, particularly when the CEO participates. In mid-sized companies, a handful of managers help carry the CEO's words into an increasingly complex operation.

In large corporations, few employees talk directly with the CEO or personally benefit from his or her vision and guidance. However, formal employee communication programs increase the odds that corporate employees understand the CEO's vision and goals. Well-orchestrated plans can also help employees feel supported and can connect them through on-the-job relationships. Large corporations typically have staff dedicated to employee communication.

The extensive research and peer-reviewed conclusions in the previously mentioned *Excellence* study did more than crystallize symmetrical and asymmetrical communication in a way that defines excellence in employee communication. In showing how getting communication right is tied to business results, the study laid a foundation for the way companies have built excellent corporate communication programs, including employee communication.[4]

The research team surveyed more than 200 people who headed communication units as well as CEOs in companies located in the U.S., Canada and the U.K. to confirm characteristics of excellent communication. The authors based their research and conclusions on companies that had a formal process and staff to implement a communication plan. While that study covered all aspects of corporate communication, it also included a chapter exclusively on employee communication and insisted a communication specialist must manage employee communication for the company to be excellent. In these organizations, it is someone's job to be the expert in employee communication.

QUESTIONS WORTH ASKING

While it is enlightening and extremely valuable, the research in *Excellence* leaves gaps. Because the research included interviews with the managers of communication units, the results reflect only companies large enough to have a communication department. Can small companies without a structured function for employee communication like those in large corporations ever rate as excellent in communication?

Or, perhaps more to the point, why should you care if small companies can have excellent employee communication when you work in a large organization?

Fair questions. And the answers cut to the heart of what corporate communicators face. You might create thoughtful and appealing communications that still don't calm people going through massive corporate upheaval or change employee behaviors so that the company can adapt to a tougher economy. How do small companies reach successful outcomes without a designated staff implementing a formal communication strategy?

This may be the best question. With the answer from this book, you will increase your value as an employee communicator, no matter the size of the company you work for.

What we've learned:

Excellent employee communication:

- Helps people establish supportive relationships on the job.
- Provides information about how their work furthers business goals.

The ways these two things are communicated typically happen differently in companies of different sizes.

Notes

1   To explore the idea of thinking in new ways:
    De Bono, E. (n.d.). New think: Preface. *Edward de Bono*. Retrieved from http://www.edwdebono.com/index.php/new-think-preface-i

2   The need for supportive relationships on the job applies not only to line workers, of course, but also to their managers:
    Rhoades Shanock, L., & Eisenberger, R. (2006). When supervisors feel supported: Relationships with subordinates' perceived supervisor support, perceived organizational support, and performance. *Journal of Applied Psychology, 91*(3), 689–695.

3   The Insync Surveys report also explores how communication about company goals and culture can improve employee retention rates.
    RedBalloon. (2010). 45% of workers plan to leave their employer within 12 months, para. 7. Retrieved from
    http://prwire.com.au/pr/25074/45-of-workers-plan-to-leave-their-employer-within-12-months

4   While the entire *Excellence* book relates to strategic communication and practices in public relations and communication, chapter 20 is on "Symmetrical Systems of Internal Communication" specifically:
    Grunig, J. E. (1992). *Excellence in public relations and communication management*. Hillsdale, New Jersey: L. Erlbaum Associates, pp. 531–575.

CHAPTER 3: APPRECIATE DIFFERENCES

Your gut might tell you that in smaller companies, the methods that lead to excellence in employee communication differ from those used in larger companies. It may seem counterintuitive at best to think that large businesses can gain from adapting best practices from their smaller counterparts.

And so we face our first step in rearranging the puzzle pieces of employee communication.

NO WORDS TO DESCRIBE IT

Corporations may use the term "employee communication" to describe keeping staff attentive to business goals and feeling connected to the culture of the company. But the term is not a concept smaller companies even recognize, particularly those with 20 or fewer employees.

According to *Thinking Big, Staying Small* (2005), for these micro-businesses—the smallest of small businesses—the concept of employee communication was completely unformed and unarticulated. Yes, the micro-business CEOs said they trained employees and listened to their input, but questions about employee communication that the researchers asked were difficult for micro-business CEOs to even answer.[1]

That's because, to them, internal communication invisibly paralleled the internal operation of the company. Despite these definitional limitations, it was clear that two-way communication for shared understanding happened this way in micro-businesses:

- CEOs are the source of employee communication.
- CEOs unconsciously communicate as part of running the business.
- Communication happens continually.
- Employees are solicited for planning input.

In a company of 20 or fewer people, the CEO essentially manages the whole business, including communication. Perhaps, then, the mid-sized group—small businesses with fewer than 500 employees but more than 20—would be more likely than micro-businesses to fit the criteria for excellent employee communication that requires a dedicated employee communication specialist and function.[2]

DEEPER DIVE

I took a deeper dive into this unstudied group of mid-sized businesses to find out about various ways to communicate effectively. Still in step with their counterpart micro-business CEOs, mid-sized company executives seldom articulate employee communication as a workplace dynamic that needs attention. They are not yet thinking about establishing an employee communication department like large businesses do, but excellent employee communication can still be investigated in these organizations. Instead of asking them how they handle employee communication, a term they might not relate with, one can observe employee communication in action in these mid-sized companies. And so I did, researching winners of the Malcolm Baldrige National Quality Award, which is given for performance improvement, quality achievement and goal attainment.[3]

The mid-sized businesses recognized with a Baldrige Award[4] were not operating with a formal communication function; however, they were communicating because, simply put, communication just happens in a workplace. People float ideas, ask questions, define value and find commonality.

Communication just happens in a workplace. People float ideas, ask questions, define value and find commonality.

Themes or patterns began to emerge. Over and over again, the ways a company shared its culture and goals were distinctive. This proved to be the case in excellent large, mid-sized and micro-businesses. All had both a culture of supportive relationships around shared values and of success in achieving goals that were tied to three dominant communication practices:

> **Shared values** are beliefs, feelings or desires that underlie the decisions or behaviors of a group.

- Communication by the CEO of the company's vision and values
- Communication integrated within operations, hardwired into processes
- Communication through internal media and programs

Perhaps even more startling and rewarding, I found evidence of balanced, symmetrical employee communication in excellent mid-sized businesses. It was being integrated with the business management process, not standing as a separate communication process the way it does in large companies. No evidence pointed to the *Excellence* study's requirement that a specialist manage the function to achieve excellence in employee communication. Not a single mid-sized company in the study indicated that responsibility for communication planning or implementation fell to a specialist. Instead, responsibility for two-way communication rested with management and all employees.

Responsibility for two-way communication rested with management and all employees.

My curiosity took me in another direction, too. As companies grow, which excellent ones are likely to do, does anything about their communication change? As it turns out, there is a sort of natural progression from micro to mid-sized to large businesses, in terms of employee communication strength. It is helpful to know where you and your company are on the path, and when to break stale patterns to freshen your communication programs. Look again:

Company size	Employee communication strength
Micro-business (up to 20 employees)	CEO as communicator through conversation about business goals and culture
Mid-sized business (21 to 500 employees)	Communication of goals and culture integrated within business operations and processes
Large business (more than 500 employees)	Consistent messages through internal "mass" media to improve understanding of strategic goals and culture

A DIFFERENT PERSPECTIVE

Here is the starting point. In a micro-business, the CEO has conversations with each individual employee, and knowing something about that employee lets him or her personalize the discussions. Because the CEO naturally and instinctively talks about vision and values, he or she passes along the corporate culture and guidance that help each individual achieve goals.

Mid-sized businesses have more employees than a CEO can reach in personal discussions. Managers, who hear directly from the CEO and then talk with their employees, take the lead in communication. Messages are about accomplishing department objectives and "the way we do things around here"—the culture of the organization.[5] That makes communication part of business operations, wired in to the routine.

Large businesses have several layers of management, which present a new challenge: consistency. When hundreds or thousands of managers are responsible for explaining the message in a way that is relevant to individual employees, a planned flow of communication can improve efficiency and effectiveness. In addition, the more people you have, the longer it takes to convey a critical message when relying strictly on managers getting around to all employees. For that reason, large companies can justify the resources to produce internal media that present consistent, strategic information and unifying cultural messages.

⭐ Soon after she began a position as the senior employee communication specialist at a large company, Courtney Sutherby reflected on the small company in Louisiana she had just left. While she did marketing communication there, no one person was in charge of employee communication. "The CEO could easily call the whole company into a conference room for a meeting, and he did at least 10 times a year. He told us stories that made us feel like we were part of a team," she said, "and he would weave in whatever announcement he had to give." The company was barely big enough to have three additional senior executives. "They knew the goals of the CEO and of the company as a whole, what the organization wanted to stand for," she said, and the executives were in the forefront talking about those things.

The small company had no employee newsletter, but it "had more people talking to each other about what was going on" than Sutherby's current employer with more than 5,000 employees in 24 U.S. states and Puerto Rico, including 600 people in one building. "One newsletter," she said, "addresses everyone as a whole." Plus, the company is developing collaborative connections online for employees who have access, which may not be possible or necessary in a small company.[6]

Communication within these two organizations is just different. Or maybe not, if we reexamine our thoughts about employee communication.

> **The following three chapters will explore the three methods of employee communication:**
> - The communicating CEO
> - Integrated operational communication, hardwired into routine processes
> - Internal media

Notes

1   Evatt, D. S., Ruiz, C., & Triplett, J. F. (2005). *Thinking big, staying small: Communication practices of small organizations*. San Francisco: International Association of Business Communicators.

2   For more information on small business characteristics and the number of employees:
    U.S. Small Business Administration. (n.d.). Firm Size Data. Retrieved from http://www.sba.gov/advocacy/849/12162

    Industry Canada. (2011). When is a business "small"? In *Key Small Business Statistics* (p. 5). Retrieved from http://www.ic.gc.ca/eic/site/061.nsf/vwapj/KSBS-PSRPE_July-Juillet2012_eng.pdf/$FILE/KSBS-PSRPE_July-Juillet2012_eng.pdf

    Enterprise and Industry. (2011). Small and medium-sized enterprises (SME): *What is an SME?* Retrieved from http://ec.europa.eu/enterprise/policies/sme/facts-figures-analysis/sme-definition/index_en.htm

3   Research and findings on employee communication among Baldrige Program winners in the small business category:
    Rosen, S. (2006). Excellence in employee communication in small companies as compared to large companies [master's thesis]. University of the Incarnate Word, San Antonio, Texas. Retrieved from http://books.google.com/books?id=nLSpECsihpUC&printsec=frontcover - v=onepage&q&f=false

4   Fewer than a hundred companies have been recognized by the *Baldrige Performance Excellence* program, and about two dozen throughout the history of the award have been mid-sized companies. The arduous award evaluation process looks at excellence in business results, strategic planning, operational processes and focus on people. The program is dedicated to raising awareness about the importance of performance excellence in driving the U.S. and global economy.
    Baldrige Performance Excellence Program. (n.d.). About Us. Retrieved from http://www.nist.gov/baldrige/about/index.cfm

5   "The way we do things around here" has been used for several decades as a working definition of corporate culture. The term seems to have originated in 1966 with Marvin Bower, a managing director for McKinsey and Company, to define business philosophy.

6   C. Sutherby, personal communication, 2011–2012.

CHAPTER 4: HEAR DIRECTLY FROM THE CEO

It's all about the CEO in a micro-business, and there's nothing wrong with that. Entrepreneurs have big ideas and strong wills, and they stay intimately involved in everything. They probably don't yet have titles for others in the company or even refer to themselves as the CEO. The 20 or fewer people who work there are just concerned with getting a chair to sit on while taking an order over the phone. At this size, a CEO talks with everyone and knows employees' interests and families through friendly, natural conversation. Each employee hears the company vision directly from the CEO. If the CEO is a good communicator, this works.

⭐ Marie Fox, the owner of a neighborhood store, dressed stylishly and stocked her elegant gift shop with chic and classic but always tasteful merchandise. She knew the women who shopped there and the men who shopped for them—maybe not individually, but she did know which designs would appeal to them. She even stocked fun, trendy items for the teenagers who passed by as they walked to or from their nearby school. She had a knack for engaging customers in a simple conversation in order to learn about them and their shopping mission—just enough to start making gift suggestions that would fit their expectations.

Most people walked into the store thinking vaguely about a gift they needed to buy but having little idea what it should be. They appreciated Marie's ideas and the stories behind particular items. And as the conversation continued, she learned more about the kind of merchandise she might add to her inventory.

RELATE PERSONALLY TO EMPLOYEES

Of course, Marie personally trained each new store employee to do the same when it came to communicating with customers. Her employees shared an understanding of how to treat people who came in and how to match each customer to the right product. Marie helped customers as well, and her employees watched her and learned by example. This way, she shared the corporate culture—how this store differentiated itself from others. It was her style, so it was also the company's style.

Each time they put a new product on the shelves, employees heard directly from the CEO about its quality and usefulness, its features and benefits. The words rolled naturally off Marie's tongue because everything about the business was important to her—but she would never have thought to call this employee communication.

LINK TO THE MARKETPLACE

Marie also asked her employees what they were hearing from customers. Did we offer what they wanted? Is there something else we should be stocking? They discussed the ways the shelves were arranged for product visibility and the flow of customer traffic through the space. The conversation wasn't a formal monthly meeting; it was part of a day's conversation. Employees knew how their interactions—not just how ringing up a sale at the register—made a difference to the business.[1]

This is an example of what *Thinking Big* [2] revealed about micro-business employee communication:

- Employees want communication from the CEO.

- Management wants employees who contribute to the company's success.

- Employees want to know how their jobs fit in and help achieve the company mission.
- Excellent employee communication is a component of excellent management processes.

It's also proof that in a micro-business, an effective CEO leads in establishing supportive relationships on the job and assures that employees have information about how their work furthers business goals.

The micro-business and the CEO are like one. "The personal objectives of owners will guide and directly influence business decisions," according to a report from the Small Business Coalition in Australia, which like the U.S. Small Business Administration, defines small business in terms of employee number, with 20 or fewer fitting its micro-business criteria.[3] A CEO is right there in the office or plant, guiding business decisions. He or she can talk confidently and competently, acting on instinct rather than any formal training, *Thinking Big* discovered. After all, these CEOs just talk about what is important to them. In one-on-one conversations, a CEO can gain employees' commitment and reinforce company values. In the smallest companies, employee communication is simply a conversation led by the CEO.

In the smallest companies, employee communication is simply a conversation led by the CEO.

A CEO like that—a confident, competent leader who explains the vision and values in terms that resonate with individual employees as if he or she were on the production floor right there with them— would be ideal in any sized business.

THE CEO'S ROLE CHANGES IN LARGER COMPANIES

But as operations grow more complex, they crowd out conversations with CEOs. Without intentional planning, larger companies will miss out on this micro-business strength.

As companies grow to the mid-sized level, most CEO conversations naturally shift to the management team, which in turn delivers the CEO's message to other employees (we'll see in the next chapter how this works in excellent companies).

In large companies, employee communication directors develop programs about company goals and culture using internal media to reach many employees. The truly personal factor disappears, and, as a result, workers pay less attention to corporate messages. To overcome this indifference, the employee communication director seeks out the CEO to deliver critical information, perhaps in town hall meetings or video messages to the entire workforce (more on this in chapter 6).

Recognizing the strength of micro-CEO conversation gives you a new pattern for shaping CEO communication wherever you might be.

CLOSING THE DISTANCE

Any time a CEO can get close and personal and make communication part of a routine, that is a step toward excellence. Ideally, a CEO would explain objectives in terms that resonate with employees, as if he or she worked in the next cubicle, as a small-business CEO can do. In a small company of virtually connected workers, though, a CEO may be located across the state or around the world from employees.

⭐ Jill Vitiello leads Vitiello Communications Group, or VTLO, headquartered in New Jersey with a virtual team of 17 consultants and staff members. The company is virtual because many of these consultants often work at the offices of their clients in different states; otherwise, they work from home. If everyone were in the same office, they would hear directly from their CEO, and they would talk among themselves to reach a shared understanding of VTLO's goals and culture as part of their daily routine. Before discovering a new, excellent approach to employee communication in this situation, Vitiello admitted, "I would communicate infrequently to the group as a whole. If I did, it was an email message to the team. That was it. There was limited opportunity for face-to-face collaboration."[4]

So while the size of this company may fall into the micro-business category, as CEO, Vitiello can't communicate with the team in person. But she can—and did—take the lead in establishing supportive relationships on the job, and assuring that employees have information about how their work furthers business goals. She now has conversations using technology in the cloud, which makes it easy for her team to connect from wherever they are.

She and her team use Chatter, a social network much like the more-familiar Facebook. This network is completely private, letting a defined group of people get answers, brainstorm ideas, share files—and reach shared understanding. It has helped her keep everyone talking to each other about business goals and the company culture as they go through their day.

EXCELLENT MANAGEMENT COMES FIRST

Virtual connections have also helped Vitiello fulfill her job as CEO more effectively. As she was growing the firm, she would work one-on-one with employees, giving them instruction or collaborating on their work. When each new employee came on board, it became harder for others to get much of her attention. "I became a bottleneck," she admitted.

It was time for a change. "I knew I had to shake things up," Vitiello said. "I challenged myself to find a different approach to enable my team to work together in real time. We have some smart, creative people on the team, so I wanted to make sure they were engaged with each other and with driving the vision for the firm."

That, she said, was the reason for turning to technology—for the ways it could improve communication. "Now, we're all more open and transparent, giving people the chance to participate or lurk as we develop relationships within the team," she said. Instead of boss and employee, VTLO is a now collaborative team.

Vitiello dips in to the scrolling news feed as her scattered team Chatters. "They aren't waiting for me to say, 'Go do it my way.'" In fact, when she posts a thought or suggests an approach, people weigh in or comment—a true, two-way conversation, not just a dictate from the leader. Whether someone is actively contributing to a particular conversation or listening and observing, the signal is clear that the CEO wants to assure clarity and understanding, the essence of excellent communication.

Communication downward, upward and sideways becomes team collaboration. "Employees have found that Chatter is the most effective way to get real-time help from each other on their projects. For example, when someone has a question or wants a second set of eyes on a document, he or she places a post on Chatter and within moments receives answers and assistance from the other employees," Vitiello said. "My employees are building strong relationships as a cohesive, connected team by working more closely together in the cloud." They are building supportive relationships with an understanding of how their work furthers business goals. The have hardwired their collaborative processes into their networked conversations.

Vitiello devotes time to participate in Chatter conversations employees have in their day-to-day routines, something she can do as the CEO of a micro-business. By necessity, though, CEOs of larger companies detach from daily operations and employee dialogue, engaging instead in conversations at a completely different level. However, wired-in communication in mid-sized businesses and internal media within large businesses can highlight the CEO as the credible leader of the company's goals and values. We'll cover those two approaches in the next few chapters.

In small companies, the CEO:

- Instinctively communicates business goals and culture through conversation in the course of a day's work.

- Can explain what needs to happen and how to do it in a personal, relevant conversation.

Though larger businesses are more complex, when the CEO talks, employees recognize that the message must be important.

Notes

1   "Marie Fox" (pseudonym), personal communication, 2003–2009.

2   Evatt, D. S., Ruiz, C., & Triplett, J. F. (2005). *Thinking big, staying small: Communication practices of small organizations*. San Francisco: International Association of Business Communicators.

3   Holmes, S., & Gibson, B. (2001). Definition of small business. Final report to the Small Business Coalition, Newcastle, Australia. p.10.

4   J. Vitiello, personal communication, 2012.

An excellent small business is not likely to remain small. Motivated, successful entrepreneurs grow companies. Eventually, structure and process interrupt personal relationships, and complexity reigns.

WHAT HAPPENED?

Jim Alampi, who owns Alampi & Associates and counsels CEOs of growing companies, says that entrepreneurs are amazed when he graphically charts how geometrically more complex a small company can become just by adding a few employees. On a white board he depicts every individual and connects each with lines to the others. A few extra people can make the web much more intricate (see below).

Growing numbers of employees increase the chance for communication disconnects

Entrepreneurs he talks with agree that the increasing number of employees, more so than increasing sales or revenues, causes disconnects in the evolution of their businesses. It's simply harder to know what everyone is doing.

THE ORGANIZATIONAL CHART IS THE FORK IN THE ROAD

"When you are below 10 employees, the CEO is intimately involved in everything," Alampi says. "To get from 10 up to 50 or 75 employees, you have to start to delegate. And you get into org. charts."[1]

The CEO begins to depend on functional managers to establish processes that simplify operations. The CEO's packed schedule precludes time for conversations with each employee, and the CEO seldom knows every employee like he or she did when the company was smaller.

NAME THAT PROBLEM

This is the point when CEOs start looking for help with something they can't clearly identify or describe. They just know something isn't quite right, or the business isn't operating as smoothly as it used to. What worked in the past doesn't any more, and frustration is high.

> **Think ahead:** Does this describe a small but growing part of your larger company, perhaps a discrete operating group or a branch office? Instead of a CEO, it may be a division manager looking to improve operations. The same guidance can apply.

Alampi has found that entrepreneurial CEOs seldom realize that the cause might be ineffective employee communication. If excellent communication were integrated into business operations, it could relieve the pressure valve of growing confusion and complexity.

> **If excellent communication were integrated into business operations, it could relieve the pressure valve of growing confusion and complexity.**

Now more than ever, the leader of a growing company needs to relearn or reinvent the way he or she shares company goals with employees and models corporate culture. What got CEOs to this point won't get them to the next. The CEO needs to delegate communication to the management team.

⭐ One CEO of a growing company who *did* identify communication as a way to relieve the pressure valve of complexity is Kip Tindell of The Container Store, a retailer of products like shelves, storage baskets and file boxes that help customers stay organized. Business was strong, more stores were built and more people were hired—but it stopped feeling like The Container Store Tindell founded. Ten years afteropening the first store in Dallas, the organization opened another one not too far away in Houston. But the distance between the two cities revealed a Texas-sized gap in the organization's culture of customer service.[2]

Tindell retold the story of transitioning from a close-knit team in the first store into complexity that arose with the second to Adam Bryant, a *New York Times* columnist:[3] "When we opened the Houston store in 1988, it was so busy that we couldn't keep up with anything." According to Tindell, they "literally didn't know what to do about it, so we called a meeting of all the employees….I wanted to be able to communicate to them what we were lacking here and how we could get it."[4]

Even he was surprised at the results aft er that one attempt to share his thoughts about "the way we do things around here"—what would become a more formally stated culture. He shared his thoughts about the philosophy of life and business that he called foundation principles, which he had collected over many years. "It was just amazing, and all anybody wanted me to do for months was just go around and talk about the foundation principles and how we apply them to our company, and how that makes us cohesive and act as a team," he said. "I began to see the incredible fierce pride that people had to work for a company that believed all these things."[5]

What Tindell experienced was the power the CEO has in moving employees to a shared understanding about how their jobs fit into a meaningful corporate purpose as well as their hunger to identify with their company's culture.

THE CEO STARTS THE CONVERSATION; MANAGERS WIRE IT IN

Since then, those first foundation principles have become Foundation Principles, trademarked and woven into the way The Container Store treats employees, customers and vendors—with respect and dignity. Tindell charged managers with making the Foundation Principles real for employees in their daily routines. The Container Store has grown to more than 3,000 employees in 30 cities, and employees' sense of contributing to the company's success and feeling supported lands the company on *Fortune* magazine's 100 Best Companies to Work For list year aft er year. The company is managed with the Foundation Principles integrated as conversation points in the daily routine.

Yet this is not an easy transition or an automatic response for a growing business. When a company grows to the point of having an organizational chart to define roles and responsibilities, the chart rarely designates an employee communication function or responsibility. In spite of this, companies that have excellent management wire communication into operations; communication becomes one of the steps employees take in completing their regular tasks. Informed, truly two-way conversation becomes part of business processes.

WIRED IN FOR SHARED UNDERSTANDING

Anyone can chart a process and include a step called communication. But integrating excellent communication into operations is more complex. It requires talking through a point so people understand and sometimes taking a different action based on the two-way discussion. That kind of excellence is evident in the companies named Baldrige Award winners for the quality processes that help them achieve business goals. These organizations demonstrate the variety of ways communication can be wired in to employees' routines.[6]

⭐ Texas Nameplate Company engraves signs for oil rigs and was one of the mid-sized companies named a Baldrige winner for small business excellence in 1998. The company had 65 employees in five departments: accounting, HR, customer service, sales and art. To ensure employees understood the business and its goals, executives gathered all 65 employees once a month to talk about progress toward the strategic plan. Even the 32 Spanish-speaking employees were present at every meeting with translators—a true commitment to communication.

Through these meetings, employees understood what the business was facing. And with that knowledge, they were invited to submit proposals for new initiatives—an aspect of two-way communication that exemplifies excellence.

⭐ Many employees want to learn more about their companies. Another mid-sized company honored with the Baldrige Award, Trident Precision Manufacturing Inc., also held employee forums for its 167 people. When employees asked to know more about progress toward goals, the company increased its network from 18 to 45 computers to give them better access to this information.

Not only were employee requests acted on, but the solution shifted the patterns of effective communication. Trident capitalized on the strengths of both small and large companies by using the small-company, face-to-face meeting style as well the large-company strength of consistent and timely media, in this case, delivered online.

⭐ When teams share an understanding of the direction of their company and the goals they are reaching for, they can connect the dots from their individual work to company success. After learning from a survey that Los Alamos National Bank workers did not understand the strategic direction of the bank or how their individual jobs contributed to the goals of their company, senior leaders took charge of communicating values and performance expectations. Los Alamos National Bank's 184 employees participated in "Breakfast with Bill" and "Snacks with Steve" programs where they were able to have conversations with their managers. These efforts resulted in greater employee understanding and the company receiving a Baldrige Award in 2000.

SO WHAT?

There's nothing so unusual about these tactics: monthly meetings with employees to discuss company goals, regular updates about progress, discussions to help employees connect the dots. Employee communication directors plan them all the time in large companies.

And that is the point. These mid-sized companies don't have employee communication directors. The people in charge of operations are also in charge of communication. They don't have PowerPoint slides with talking points crafted by an employee communication staff.

Recall what *Excellence* said: "Such variables as motivation, leadership and productivity affect the way people communicate in an organization."[7] In a company with poor management, communication will likely fail at creating motivation or productivity. Excellent management comes first so that excellent employee communication can be integrated into the daily operations of excellent corporations.

⭐ And it works, even as companies add employees. Excellent managers with communication wired in to daily operations can continue their success as the company grows. Sunny Fresh Foods Inc., a wholly owned subsidiary of Cargill Inc., made the Baldrige list first in 1999 with 380 employees, called stakeholders. Its Leadership System charted six requirements. The first was to listen, and the second was to communicate the core purpose and clear values. Also on the list were the operational expectations of managers to discuss progress toward goals with employees. Sunny Fresh Foods won again in 2005 with 620 employees in the large-business category. With the second entry, Sunny Fresh Foods reported that 90 percent of its employees agreed with the survey statements "I understand the goals of Sunny Fresh" and "I understand how my job affects the customer."

GIVING EMPLOYEE COMMUNICATION ITS NAME

Even without a department in charge of employee communication, mid-sized companies recognize the concept. Remember, in the case of micro-businesses, CEOs did not recognize the terminology well enough to answer questions about their employee communication practices.

⭐ Park Place Lexus, the 2005 Baldrige small-business winner, stood out as purposefully integrating two-way symmetrical communication into operations, even to the extent of actually calling it employee communication—at least as a process, though not a staffed function. The management team charted employee communication methods (below), and a few of the methods make the point that two-way communication is expected. Communicating with employees, who the company calls "members," is part of operational processes that are guided by the leadership team.[8]

Park Place Lexus   **Leadership**

Method	Frequency	2-way	Target Members	What is Communicated
Strategy Deployment Meeting	Annual	Yes	All Members	Directions, Changes, Values, Expectations
Review Meetings (*Figure 4.1C*)	As shown	Yes	All Members – Various Meetings	Directions, Performance, Issues & Concerns, Recognition
Bulletin Boards	Ongoing	No	All Members	Job information, Performance, Values
Process Documents	Ongoing	No	All Members	Expectations, Changes to Process, Procedures
Team Park Place	Monthly	Yes	All Members	Performance, Recognition, Directions
Q12 survey	Annual	No	All Members	Upward Communication of Satisfaction
Experts in Excellence Workshop	On Going	Yes	All Members	Directions, Expectations
Foundations (New Hire Orientation)	On Hire	Yes	All New Hires	Directions, Values, Expectations
PPU - Online	Ongoing	No	All Members	Training Opportunities
Open Door Policy	Ongoing	Yes	All Members	Any Area of Concern
Exit Interviews	As Needed	Yes	All Terminated	Concerns, Reasons for Leaving
Member Performance Reviews	Annual	Yes	All Members	Directions, Values, Expectations, Performance, Development Opportunities
Committee Participation (MAC, 50/50, etc)	Varies	Yes	Committee Members	Satisfaction, Directions, Client Focus, Performance, Opportunities
Suggestion Boxes		No	All Members	Ideas and Suggestions

Figure 1.1B – Employee Communication and Deployment Methods

This chart identifies specific topics for dialogue as part of operational processes. One of these methods was called 50/50 communication meetings, which are monthly open forums focused 50 percent on ideas and concerns and 50 percent on solutions. Any of the 365 employees could attend. In addition, the annual strategic plan was explained to all employees through deployment meetings. "This meeting is used to communicate not only the…direction, but each member's role and responsibilities in attaining our goals," Park Place reported.[9]

SOLVE PROBLEMS TOGETHER

If all this sounds like just another boring meeting, especially if you are used to the corporate world with a calendar full of meetings, think about how different the agenda of one of these operational meetings can be. A manager close to the CEO talks about what the executive leadership is thinking. It becomes a direct conversation about what that actually means to you. Throughout the conversation, you have a chance to offer comments, opinions and suggestions that will determine how you and the company operate.

Research from the U.K. sheds light on how this kind of meeting exchange differs from mid-sized to large companies. The Policy Studies Institute in London studied mid-sized companies with 25 to 200 employees to determine how effective communication can boost financial performance (and indeed it did). This research confirmed that what works in large companies is different from what works in small companies, mostly because of bureaucracy. It also supports the notion that operational communication is the strength of mid-sized companies.[10]

In particular, the study confirms the value of team briefings. Briefings bring management and employees together to ask and answer questions, much like the practices of Baldrige winners in the U.S. Teams share in problem-solving and decision-making. There is an added benefit to this type of communication, according to the Policy Studies Institute. Direct communication with employees is not only more effective at reaching shared understanding, but it is also less expensive than the more formal methods larger companies use. In settings like these, employees listen to management so they can make informed suggestions when it is their turn to talk—when conversation becomes problem-solving.

In mid-sized businesses, no communication professional needs to position messages to keep employees on track in attaining business goals or to make sure they understand marketplace pressures so they can respond to customers. No trained communicator acts on employee input in shaping communication plans or advising senior executives about the communication-related implications of their decisions. There are no award-winning media or creative, engaging campaigns to capture attention.

And yet, many mid-sized companies succeed.

Communication is integrated with the business management process, not necessarily a communication process or department unto its own.

> **Communication is integrated with the business management process, not necessarily a communication process or department unto its own.**

Mid-sized businesses are not just overgrown micro-businesses, nor are they smaller versions of big companies. They have their own excellent employee communication strength, a specifically valuable communication approach: integrating dialogue into operations—wiring-in communication as part of daily departmental activities. This is an effective way to talk about company goals and share the way to do things, the culture of the business. Also, as part of operational conversations, employees share their observations with their managers, which is important for planning and improvements. Responsibility for two-way communication rests with all management and all employees.

CREATING A CULTURE ON A BLANK PIECE OF PAPER

⭐ Pro-Tec Coating Company jumped right in at the mid-sized company level with the entrepreneurial sensibility of a small company and the acquired wisdom of a large corporation. Established as a joint venture between U.S. Steel and Kobe Steel, it started production in 1993 with a mission to foster human potential, a spirit of cooperation and technical innovation. Pro-Tec systematically wired communication into operations and people management, from top to bottom, to help employees connect the dots between their work and company success.

Like a micro-business, the president of Pro-Tec annually reports business results to all associates—the inclusive term it uses for its 231 employees. In informal meetings, he talks with employees about whatever they are interested in discussing. But this is, after all, a mid-sized business, so he delegates responsibility for communicating his vision as "a more concrete picture of what the company will look like in 10 years" to his seven direct reports.[11] That picture comes into focus in leadership team conversations around these points: How can we foster human potential? What does the spirit of cooperation look like? Where will technical innovation take us? Sometimes you have to ask questions to pull people into a conversation, and it can be as simple as asking what they think.

> **Tip:** Ask people a genuine question to make it a two-way exchange that can clarify or confirm a thought. It can be as simple as asking what they think. Then be present and listen for context in the answers. Questions and answers can happen in face-to-face meetings, as part of job processes, and in formal media.

The vision and mission show up again in department and team meetings when, as employees make a tactical decision, a team leader commonly asks, "What do our mission and vision say about this?" As individuals learn about their tasks, they also learn culture—which specifically for Pro-Tec is the value of ownership, responsibility and accountability. In the middle of doing work, conversations provide support and connect tasks to goals.

Even internal mass media show up at Pro-Tec, something borrowed from the organization's large-business parent companies. Every employee knows how goals specific to his or her position are linked with balanced scorecard goals, and those numbers are readily available on the company intranet. Along with operational news, achievements are published in a quarterly newsletter or appear on closed circuit television to support the culture of ownership, responsibility and accountability.

"Our desire is to have every Associate connect what he or she does on a daily basis to the goals of the company," Pro-Tec stated in its Baldrige application. "We strive to create an environment that fosters involvement, participation, and ownership of the plan by communicating the goals and identifying the linkage between goals and individual Associate activities."[12] Leaders are in charge of making that link, and to do that, Pro-Tec insists that all leaders are good listeners and communicators. They know it works because they measure it. And in 2007, the Baldrige Performance Excellence program named Pro-Tec Coating Company a winner.

YES, BUT...

Delegating communication responsibility for vision, culture and goals to the management team is a step toward wiring in communication, and during financially stressful or competitive times, it is essential. Line managers who connect personally with employees can help interpret any company upheaval and provide support. This doesn't always work, though. Different managers have varying degrees of competency in linking concepts like core values and mission to tangible, specific tasks in operations. To make matters worse, some employees may not be engaged or be paying attention, tuning out unless the story is told to create meaning for them.

In large companies, employee communication directors guide multiple layers of managers, who must tackle the unending tasks of giving people the support they seek and explaining how their work fits into the big picture. Also, communication directors in large companies can send consistent messages directly to employees through internal media in case managers stray in telling the company story. Creative campaigns can win back people's attention. That is the next level, the employee communication strength of large companies, which we explore in the next chapter.

What we've learned about mid-sized companies' communication strength:

With a substantial number of workers comes confusion and complexity in operations. Companies with excellent management integrate two-way dialogue into business processes to:

- Establish supportive relationships on the job.
- Provide information about how employees' work furthers business goals.

When managers take the lead in balanced, symmetrical communication, conversations happen at the team level. Teams can share in problem-solving and decision-making:

- They share the meaning of their endeavors (information about how their work furthers business goals).
- They learn how to make things happen together (establish supportive relationships on the job).

Notes

1   J. Alampi, personal communication, 2004.

2   Bryant, A. (2010, March 13). Three good hires? He'll pay more for one who's great. *The New York Times*. Retrieved from http://www.nytimes.com/2010/03/14/business/14corners.html?pagewanted=all

3   Bryant, para. 22.

4   Bryant, para. 23.

5   Bryant, para. 25.

6   All Baldrige winner profiles mentioned in this chapter are available to the public at:
    Baldrige Performance Excellence Program. (n.d.). Award recipients' contacts and profiles. Retrieved 1 October 2011, from http://www.baldrige.nist.gov/Contacts_Profiles.htm

7   Grunig, J. E. (1992). *Excellence in public relations and communication management*. Hillsdale, New Jersey: L. Erlbaum Associates, p. 548.

8   Park Place Lexus. (2005). 2005 Baldridge Performance Excellence Study award recipient application summary. Retrieved from http://www.baldrige.nist.gov/2005_Application_Summaries.htm

9   Park Place Lexus, p. 2.

10 Policy Studies Institute. (1998, October 28). *Direct communication with employees boosts small firms' financial performance*. Retrieved from http://www.psi.org.uk/press/Abpress.htm

11 Pro-Tec Coating Company. (2007). 2007 Malcolm Baldrige application summary. Retrieved from http://www.baldrige.nist.gov/2007_Application_Summaries.htm

12 Pro-Tec Coating Company, p. 2.

CHAPTER 6: VALUE CONSISTENCY

Who invented employee communication anyway? Hundreds, perhaps thousands, of people forged the first significant modern employee communication artifact—the company internal publication. By the last half of the 20th century, many companies published elaborate, elegant and effective magazines for their employees. But that turned out to be just a passing phase, a tactic in what was to become a much broader discipline that expanded focus from a product to ongoing patterns of useful communication.

INTERNAL JOURNALISTS

⭐ Roger D'Aprix and John Gerstner were part of a wave of writers who shaped employee communication into a defined practice. They knew how to get the word out—to tell the company's story—at a time when corporations gained so many new faces that some form of communication to the masses became absolutely necessary. The U.S. workforce was growing rapidly, and companies bulged with baby boomers. Workers needed to know what was going on with their employers.

Many of these companies already had public relations departments, typically staffed by former newspapermen whose friendships with current reporters worked to the company's advantage. Junior public relations staffers often were assigned to produce employee publications. Even before that, something akin to an infant employee communication discipline was recognized in some progressive personnel departments, what we currently call human resources or employee relations. Roger D'Aprix, who foresaw the value of connecting workplace discussion with marketplace context, tells of joining General Electric in 1959 as a writer and hearing the head of employee relations organizing a meeting of communicators. "What in the world, I thought, is a communicator? He might just as well have told me that he had scheduled a meeting of breathers," D'Aprix wrote. "What he was doing, it turned out, was organizing a gathering of the people who were responsible for the various employee publications at G.E. so they could confer about their common challenges, tasks and problems."[1]

When General Motors, the poster child for big business at the time, created its first centralized employee communication function in 1972 to put some rigor to the process, several GM plants already had publications. Early examples of employee publications were likely to be compilations of submissions from employees about personal accomplishments and family news or documentation of happenings around the company. Another early example, IBM's *Think* magazine, was first issued in 1935 for employees and customers. Its content included thought pieces by academics, scientists, politicians and business leaders—as well as an article about IBM's values explained by its CEO, Thomas J. Watson Sr.[2]

Deere & Company appreciated having good writers on its staff. It already published a high-quality magazine for farm customers and rural communities, *The Furrow*, that reported on agriculture topics. John Gerstner, then a regional editor for *The Furrow*, was charged in 1975 with launching another magazine, the *John Deere Journal*. This one was specifically for employees and retirees along with external influencers, including educators, legislators and community leaders.

"The vision was to produce a quality publication that reflected the achievements, goals and aspirations of the publisher," said Gerstner, positioning it miles apart from companies where a secretary might collect snippets about employees to compile in a multi-page flier.[3] While Gerstner's was among the best, the *Journal* was certainly not the only well-funded corporate employee publication of that era.

Companies around the world were creating employee communication departments to produce media as a way of reaching a large number of people internally.

> ## Companies around the world were creating employee communication departments to produce media as a way of reaching a large number of people internally.

FROM COPYCAT PUBLISHING TO BEST PRACTICES

With employees as the target readers, writers like Gerstner, or industrial editors as they were called for a while, wrote news and feature articles; took or commissioned breathtaking photography; relied on well-paid graphic designers; followed strict editorial schedules with content planned months in advance; and published on giant, four-color presses. This was pure publishing, just like their magazine counterparts in mass media, only without paid advertising. But was it employee communication?

"In the 1970s and up to the mid-1980s, there wasn't an established set of best-practices for employee communication," said Gerstner, who today runs his own company, Communitelligence, which helps communicators keep up with the best in corporate communication trends and strategies.

In those earlier days, well-written and well-designed were adjectives that never meant much to accountants and business managers balancing budgets during one economic downturn or another. The content didn't justify scarce dollars, whether in-depth articles about current events in the industry, profiles of major customers or human-interest features. The publications may have been interesting, they may have even given employees a sense of pride in their company, but for executives controlling expenses, these things were expendable. Communication directors had to better justify their work. Some didn't succeed, and many employee magazines were eliminated.

STRENGTH IN CONSISTENT MESSAGE

Mini recessions every decade or so were just a taste of what was ahead in the Great Recession much of the world is navigating now. Over the years, through the economic fog, the appropriate justification for funding employee publications seemed a bit muted, but the justification was there all along. As discussed in the previous chapter, in the progression from a micro-sized business to a mid-sized business, managers take charge of the communication responsibility from the CEO. But in moving from a mid-sized organization to a large company, it can become a hindrance to rely on managers as communicators. More organizational layers add to the likelihood of inconsistent messages being delivered—and sometimes managers aren't even accountable for delivering corporate messages at all.

The real value of corporate media, it turns out, was in delivering a consistent message to reach a large group of employees at the same time. When everyone needs simultaneous and quick access to the message, mass media are far superior to taking the time for managers to cascade information down multiple levels of the company, risking the message being reinterpreted and revised along the way.

When everyone needs simultaneous and quick access to the message, mass media are far superior to taking the time for managers to cascade information down multiple levels of the company, risking the message being reinterpreted and revised along the way.

In between recessions, corporations had flush times. Employee communication departments and their mass media benefited. Some companies, notably Federal Express, now FedEx, invested in in-house video production and satellite distribution in the 1980s.[4] An internal staff could deliver visual and emotional messages, video's advantage, with the same consistency and immediacy of print. Then came the Internet, and on its heels, intranets. Employee communication directors learned to integrate multiple media to work in tandem, measuring which worked best for different purposes.

⭐ Today, employee communicators at MD Anderson Cancer Center reach out to employees with well-orchestrated audio podcasts, blogs, video, print and online newsletters targeted by audience. They also hold live question-and-answer chat sessions with executives and experts; produce an award-winning color magazine; and hold small-group, face-to-face meetings and large town halls. And the list goes on. "We use everything," said Laura Harvey, director for internal communications. "Even tried and true communication methods, such as posting fliers on bulletin boards."[5]

The 20,000 employees and volunteers are busy caring for patients or supporting those who care for patients. "We have passionate people dedicated to Making Cancer History®, which really is our mission. Everyone knows why they're here—it's patients first," Harvey said. As they rush through their day, one of their individually preferred media will be there at a time they can take note of it. "We're reaching four or five generations, and we understand our people have different ways to digest information," she said. In an institution where work can feel so overwhelming and sometimes truly is a life-or-death situation, pushing information to employees requires brevity, creativity and even humor, where appropriate.

Any integrated media mix can deliver consistent information in a way that takes advantage of the medium, but the mix is not about repetition. For example, while an intranet includes far more information than a publication, print complements online notices by providing context or interpretation. Some people prefer to watch a video, while others listen to a podcast during their commute. While the best videos and podcasts don't share a script, they do share terms, giving employees a common language to describe their company and daily work. Whatever the media—print, online or video—all options bump up against the same problem, what marketers call mindshare and the Webster dictionary defines as "time spent thinking about something." Too many messages vie for employees' limited time; thus the need for a strategic communication plan that prioritizes messages.

Too many messages vie for employees' limited time; thus the reason for a strategic communication plan that prioritizes messages.

A strategic communication plan is something a professional communicator in the employee communication function handles with the company's executive team, just like the groundbreaking *Excellence* study expected. As D'Aprix, one of the founding fathers of employee communication practices, wrote in *Communicating For Change*: "The real challenge in communicating with employees is to create a careful strategy…rather than…a collection of fragmented programs and messages all competing for attention and leaving the employee audience to figure out what it all means."[6] Employee communication directors can use the most effective media they manage and blend them to impart meaning to employees. Without lapsing into repetition, the message remains consistent, and all employees have access to the same explanation.

Employees at MD Anderson won't pay attention to all of the media available to them, but the hope is that will they hear or see the essential point. "People not only receive messages from us, but from everyone on the planet. We have to focus on the ones of real importance, what truly is in line with our goals," Harvey said. "The hardest part is prioritizing to stay aligned with business goals."

The MD Anderson communication team manages consistency in message with a core document on each priority topic or issue. From that source document, all the writers, producers, or content managers craft a message in the appropriate way for the medium and for the target audience. With identified priorities and the shared core document, what matters most is consistently at hand so the right message can rise above the cacophony.

When the same message is packaged the best way for each medium, employees can choose the channel they prefer.

IS CONSISTENCY THE SAME AS EXCELLENCE?

Communication directors know how easy media budgets are to cut. Our ongoing task is to convince management of the importance of employee communication in helping employees establish supportive relationships on the job and learn about how their work furthers business goals. These two factors set the foundation for employee engagement, and that affects the bottom line. Communication directors who help executives understand this value will survive the upheaval of this global recession.

Survival alone doesn't equal excellence, though.

Keep in mind that employee communication must be symmetrical to be excellent, which at the time the *Excellence* study was completed—before digital interactive media—was much more difficult. Even now, traditional internal mass media easily slide into

> **Remember:** Excellent communication uses dialogue for clarity and confirmation.

asymmetrical communication as persuasion to achieve business goals or tell the corporate story. Excellent communication requires a dialogue to improve understanding of the root issue. To share meaning, truly listening to each other is vitally important. Only through the give and take of conversation with employees can you, the communicator or executive, find out if people feel supported on the job or understand how their work furthers business goals. Mass media's job is to reinforce this understanding and shared meaning.

TODAY'S TWO-WAY TOOLS

Today, mass communication includes tools like Twitter, YouTube, Pinterest, Google+, Facebook, and their global counterparts, as well as whatever was released last week and rose to the buzz level yesterday. Two-way communication, right? These tools can at least be a chance to listen to what your audience is saying and join in.

John Gerstner sees a genuine attempt by serious communicators to use these tools to look beyond the role of only managing messages and media. They are opening channels that allow listening and dialogue. "The most interesting and exciting developments are happening when we empower employees to become content creators themselves, via employee blogs, comments on intranet articles, wikis and online videos. This allows them to easily share ideas and collaborate both internally and with those outside the company—using the whole array of social media tools including blogs, instant messaging, web conferencing, Twitter, Yammer, Facebook and LinkedIn," Gerstner said.

With this evolution, employee communication directors are discovering or rediscovering the power of conversation that naturally happens in the workplace. Recall that people float ideas, ask questions, define value and find commonality, with or without a formal communication plan.

"As one example, a company I consult for publishes articles on its intranet homepage blog that regularly spark dozens of comments. The most common comments are questions about some facet of the article that wasn't covered. Invariably, other employees from all over the organization will give answers to the questions, all without any mediation by internal communicators," Gerstner said. "That's powerful."

Exchanges like these can establish supportive relationships on the job and help people get information about how their work fits in and furthers business goals.

IS AN EMPLOYEE COMMUNICATOR STILL NEEDED?

And where is the employee communication specialist, considered a requirement for excellence in large companies, in all of this online dialogue? Still keeping the enterprise message in front of everyone.

That's because friends and fans and connections of loosely gathered employees could be having conversations on just about anything. If you embrace the value of symmetrical two-way communication as well as the importance of communities within the larger employee base, you can encourage dialogue for shared meaning around the things that matter most in the company (we look at communities and their dialogue in the following chapters).

Is a consistent message still needed?

Henry Ford's quip that a "customer can have a car painted in any color that he wants so long as it is black" didn't last for Ford Motor Company. One size doesn't fit all, and there is a limit to uniformity in internal media to the masses. Even consumer mass media, which employee communicators often mimicked, developed versions for different demographics. Magazines printed different covers for submarkets, and newspapers printed regional editions. Fast forward to today; current communication technology capabilities make customization and personalization of news and information a choice of the *receiver*, not the sender.

If employees can choose the online tools they use to interact with colleagues and to find out more about their work, do employee communication directors still have a role? With all of the individual, separate digital discussions, how can employee communication directors promote consistency in message? Is this even possible in a workforce splintered by age, location and language, not to mention media preference?

It's not hopeless, but hold on for a wild ride.

The role of the employee communication director is evolving into one that puts voice to what unites us, not facilitating splinter conversations.

The role of the employee communication director is evolving into one that puts voice to what unites us, not facilitating splinter conversations. We are reinventing employee communication plans and tactics as we recognize changes in our amorphous employee audience. Audience does not equal community, and communities are the direction social media are taking us—communities that establish supporting relationships on the job.

Communities are now the other side of balanced, symmetrical communication—sometimes even both receiver and sender. As employee communication director, you can still guide dialogue on topics that matter most to the company, and do so with consistency. To help build community and personal connections among employees, communicators for large companies can adapt techniques from small and mid-sized businesses.

Consider this progression of employee communication in large companies:

- Internal publications delivered consistent messages to all employees at the same time.

- Employee communication grew beyond the boundaries of print, developing strategies to integrate multiple media and to give priority to certain messages.

- By financial necessity, employee communicators develop plans and programs to help employees establish supportive relationships on the job and get information about how their work fits in and further business goals.

- With technology tools, employees now more easily connect and converse, outside of any formal communication plan or produced media. The mass employee audience may be disappearing from mass internal media as social media take us in a different direction.

- A new role for employee communicators is emerging, one of guiding the dialogue of communities inside the larger employee audience. This still involves prioritizing messages and promoting consistency. It remains about excellent, two-way symmetrical communication.

Notes

1   D'Aprix, R. (n.d.). The evolution of organizational communication. In *Internal communication: A comprehensive manual for professionals who communicate with today's employees* (Vol. 1). Chicago: Ragan Communications Inc., p. 9.

2   Though not many histories are written about the employee communication discipline, the following include references to early employee publications and programs:
(2001). Executive briefing: Retired General Motors communication director tells how to pull your company out of the Stone Age. *Journal of Employee Communication Management*, July/August, 9–13.
IBM100: A Culture of Think. (n.d.). Retrieved from http://www.ibm.com/ibm100/us/en/icons/think_culture/transform/
Reuss, C., & Silvis, D. E. (1985). Inside organizational communication (2nd ed.). New York City: Longman.

3   J. Gerstner, personal communication, 2010–2012.

4   Read more about early corporate video programs:
    Associated Press. (1988, July 1). Private television networks grow as businesses turn to satellite video. *The Los Angeles Times*.
    Retrieved from http://articles.latimes.com/1988-07-01/business/fi-6531_1_private-satellite-network

5   L. Harvey, personal communication, 2012.

6   D'Aprix, R. (1996). *Communicating for change*. San Francisco: Jossey-Bass, p. xxi.

CHAPTER 7: STEP OUTSIDE YOUR BOX

It is possible in micro and even mid-sized small businesses to have a meaningful two-way exchange with employees. Is it realistic to expect a large business to make conversation an intentional part of an employee communication plan? To help you envision how small-style communication could work consistently throughout a large company, consider Alpha Natural Resources. That company moved through the stages from a micro to mid-sized to large business rapidly, and with each step, it found its footing using and reusing strengths in conversation, operational, and media communication as the size of its audience and the needs of the company changed.

⭐ In true entrepreneurial style, everything started with an idea. The founder of Alpha Natural Resources, its first CEO, had no polished or published 10-point business plan, but he had friends. They understood his vision for the company to acquire coal operations around Appalachia, and he had faith in those first employees to make it happen. They moved pieces of furniture from their individual homes to set up an office in Abingdon, Virginia. They shared an understanding of the possibilities. The initial public offering occurred just three years later.

The company started with four employees in 2001, and by 2009, the count was nearly 3,600. That's when the company was preparing for a major acquisition that would nearly double its size, making it the third largest coal company in the United States, operating 74 mines and plants with 6,400 employees.

The nature of the business requires teamwork and attention to safety. On those two essentials, the company's core values and communication efforts rest. You might wonder what kind of culture you can have in a dark, dirty, dangerous, demanding worksite like a coal mine. A mine is a confined environment, like a stage, and operations must be orchestrated like an "underground ballet," to use Ted Pile's term.[1] He is Alpha's vice president of corporate communication.

After two serious accidents, the company executives took time to reflect. They knew that 90 percent of workplace accidents are caused by human behavior. They decided to put the power to keep the workplace safe into the hands of the people who worked in the mines. They called it Running Right.

COMMUNICATION IS EVERYONE'S RESPONSIBILITY

Running Right assigns each employee the role of identifying and addressing at-risk behaviors—with no retribution. In a precarious coal mine, everyone has to watch out for each other. That feeling of being part of a protective family gives any employee not only the right but also the responsibility to speak up if he sees something questionable and say, "let me help you pick up that heavy object," or "remember to use your safety gloves," or "make sure you tag and lock out before working on electrical equipment."

Guidance comes from the top. "I don't want anyone's life changed [for the worse] because they were here trying to earn a living for their family.... Whenever we have an injury, families are impacted," Alpha's founder and chairman Mike Quillen said.

Guidance also comes from the bottom. Employees were speaking up about ways to keep everyone safe at work using simple, small observation cards that were bringing in 10,000 to 12,000 ideas—each month. The suggestion program is localized, mine by mine, and best practices are shared across the company. It's proof of a culture of safety deeply rooted in operations. Together, a team of hourly and salaried employees looks at each one of those suggestions. Some can be acted on immediately. Some require work plans. But every suggestion is considered.

Though Alpha has grown beyond micro and even mid-sized to be a large business, it still makes time for conversation in operational communication as part of a planned communication strategy. Precisely because the company leaders recognize employee communication as the lubricant of a well-run machine, conversation and operational communication stay strong at a point when other companies might have relied instead on efficient and consistent internal media. Everyone has a voice in safety, and everyone has a responsibility to communicate the corporate culture of safety.

TAKE ACTION BY LEARNING FROM THE STRENGTHS OF OTHER-SIZED COMPANIES

You don't have to operate only within your box based on your size and associated, traditional strength. If you lead employee communication in a large company, embrace your strength in media, but don't blindly rely on media only. Envision other communication options by piecing together ideas borrowed from businesses of other sizes. You greatly expand your options for communication excellence when you understand how micro-businesses communicate culture and how mid-sized companies exhibit their strength in communicating strategy—the direction of the company as evident in its vision and mission. Let's step through this detailed look:

Communication strengths vary by the size of the company, but your company's size doesn't limit your opportunities

	Conversation	Operational communication	Media
Micro small business	Strength in strategy	Opportunity for strategy	Opportunity for culture
Mid-sized business	Opportunity for culture	Strength in strategy	Opportunity for strategy
Large business	Opportunity for culture	Opportunity for strategy	Strength in strategy and culture

Employee Communication Strength and Opportunity by Company Size © Sheri Rosen, 2016, and licensed under Creative Commons for you to use, share and build upon with attribution to Sheri Rosen

Locate your "size box" in the first column. How are you capitalizing on the strength that comes with a company the size of yours? Look along that row to see where you have additional opportunities for excellence in communication strategy or culture. Are your opportunities in conversation, operational communication or media?

Employee communication in micro-businesses is simply conversation. A CEO has the vision that creates meaning for others, and together they develop the strategy and build a culture.

When the company grows beyond the CEO's ability to have that kind of personal relationship with everyone, discussion about strategy and culture—when done right—is wired in to the actual operations of the company.

Large companies have good reason to use media to explain strategy and culture efficiently to a large number of employees. Yet there's always opportunity in communicating the way micro and mid-sized business do.

> **Large companies have good reason to use media to explain strategy and culture efficiently to a large number of employees. Yet there's always opportunity in communicating the way micro and mid-sized businesses do.**

All it takes is to recognize that there are, in fact, valid models for doing so. Whether intentionally planned or by chance, when employees in large companies talk among themselves, they share the meaning of their endeavors. That is also true when conversation is with the head of the company as in a micro-business or within work groups in mid-sized companies. And it is true across generations.

In conversation, people talk about "the way we do things around here"—Running Right, in the case of Alpha Natural Resources.

EMBED A TOPIC IN OPERATIONAL CONVERSATION

As it turned out at Alpha, everyone had a chance to define the mission, which drives goals, grounded in the values they experience each day at work. In this young company, executives and consultants penned a working mission in a closed conference room in 2009 after the merger that thrust the company to mining prominence. The words stressed the importance of stabilizing the company. It was a short-term mission, though. One year later, the time was right for an aspirational statement, and in the Running Right way, every employee had a voice in its writing.

Since the culture is foremost about safety and looking out for each other, 15 trained facilitators were already holding regular Running Right meetings in the field to prioritize safety issues and suggestions as a way to show that the company cared for everyone and wanted to keep them safe. Facilitators also were leading teambuilding as employees joined Alpha from different corporate cultures to be oriented to Running Right. Communication was already wired in to operations.

Ted Pile and his communication team only needed to add a topic for conversation, and then listen.

They developed a toolkit for these facilitators to seek out information from all employees so Alpha could create a new mission for the growing company from the grassroots up. They held listening sessions within mine operations. In places where listening sessions were not feasible, or people were unable to fill out paper surveys—sometimes even because an individual didn't know how to write—facilitators walked alongside miners as they worked and captured their responses to just a few questions.

Pile and the communication team even gave the facilitators pocket video cameras to record individual employees explaining their thoughts. The compilation of those videos created a compelling story about how the final version of the mission was, in fact, what employees envisioned. "We wanted miners to have a say in our future," Pile said.

In compiling the results of the listening efforts, five themes emerged: safety, family, leaders who walk the talk, pride in working hard—and please make the vision simpler and plainer.

Here was the previous version of the mission:

"Our near-term mission is to maximize the opportunities and benefits of combining our two organizations. We will do this by (i) achieving a seamless and timely integration, (ii) fully stabilizing the new organization, and (iii) executing on our business plan so we begin to reach our full potential by year-end 2009."

And the new, employee-powered mission:

"We power the world through the energy of our people."

In the Running Right way, Pile took the new version back to the facilitators to find out whether a sample of employees understood it. Employees raved. Now, the mission is in front of them every day, visible to them on their co-workers' hardhats—a version of mass media you've probably never thought of.

WHEN THE CEO TALKS, PEOPLE NOTICE

The real launch of the new mission came, appropriately, from the CEO and his executive team. The CEO wrote about it in his blog, which doesn't reach the mines. So paper copies were posted there. The headline was "Your fingerprints are on our future," a fitting image as coal-stained hands had left fingerprints on the paper surveys many miners filled out during the research and listening phase of the mission development.

Your finger prints are on our future

A year ago, we were in the midst of amazing times. Right as we were passing through one of the biggest global financial collapses in world history, Alpha Natural Resources

Alpha Natural Resources CEO Kevin Crutchfield went on to say in his blog that he had listened to employees, and he invited them to post comments—continuing the conversation like a micro-business CEO strengthening strategy and culture.[2]

In addition, executives met with employees at 25 sites within three days, as the new mission was unveiled. Local leaders met with more employees at additional sites. The management team showed cohesion in the new mission and appreciation to the employees who gave it meaning. Employees noticed. "In surveys we did, one thing that always came across was the value of executive leaders just showing up. It was that simple—showing up between shifts and shaking hands," Pile said. "I think the people liked knowing that our executives were interested enough in them to ask them questions."

These conversations make employees feel like they are supported on the job, and it personalizes the information about how their work furthers business goals.

Running Right depends equally on all employees, not only management employees, to achieve success. In a sense, when we call one group "employees" and another group "management," we can easily forget that "manager" is merely another flavor of "employee." Alpha executives weren't fooled. "Our guys are good at saying, 'We work for you. You are the backbone of the company,'" Pile explained.

Responsibility for excellent, two-way communication rests with all managers and all employees.

Is it possible that putting the power and responsibility for Running Right into the hands of miners might have prevented the worst U.S. mining disaster in decades? A West Virginia mine operated by a different company, Massey Energy, exploded deep underground in 2010, killing 29 people. The company, it turned out, had a history of safety violations. The disaster brought federal investigations, the resignation of Massey's CEO and lawsuits. A little more than a year after the explosion, Alpha Natural Resources acquired Massey Energy in June 2011, again doubling its size.

THE COMPANY CHANGES, AGAIN

Combined, the number of Alpha employees was 14,000. That adds up to a lot of new people who must find shared meaning in Running Right. Of course, nobody is holding employees responsible for all safety. "There's a clear chain of responsibility for safety in the mines that includes mine management, business unit management, our VP of safety and health, right on up to our executive leadership," Pile explained.

Nonetheless, Running Right is being instilled with each new employee through face-to-face team sessions about safety processes and training. In the first three months following the acquisition, 63,000 staff hours of training were devoted to instilling the cultural principles of Running Right among Massey's 7,000-plus employees.

"This was a total eye-opener for former Massey employees, who were accustomed to a top-down system. Now, it was bottom up—everyone has a seat at the table and a voice in safety," Pile said. The former Massey employees were being acculturated into Alpha to learn new behaviors, on-site, with their teams, face to face, complimented by internal media such as bulletin boards and email for those with access.

You can be sure there was hesitancy, confusion and fear among employees moving into a new company from one with so many questions still swirling around after the disaster. But the results of empowering the workforce from Massey through Running Right have been immediate and impressive. Within five months of the acquisition, the former Massey employees were turning in more Running Right observation cards than the legacy Alpha employees were. In total, 30,000-plus ideas now come in every month from the combined workforce. And the former Massey mines had improved their safety performance by double digits.

However, not only the mineworkers—the employees—are learning the culture of their new company. Today's managers are a mix of Alpha and Massey people. To unite these 220 managers, the Alpha CEO used both mid-sized and large business approaches. Acting like a mid-sized business, managers heard about culture and strategy directly from the CEO so they could talk with their employees about goals and give support. Acting like a large business with several layers of management all needing clarity and involvement, Alpha held a two-day leadership summit.

The agenda covered values and vision. There were no slides about the business or financial results. Instead, the summit included team exercises to further promote understanding, connection and dialogue. They evaluated the desires and fears of employees. Participants were encouraged to speak up, sharing thoughts via iPads throughout the sessions that were projected for everyone to see. The CEO read them and asked questions. They brainstormed ways to achieve their stated purpose. They used scenarios to practice problem-solving and decision-making. In the end, they learned more about themselves and each other.

"We've empowered many more of our leaders to take our message out, and we've provided talking points, FAQs, and video to use based on their situations, whether a pre-shift meeting or a business unit office meeting. We have PowerPoint designed for an office setting or a two-sided handout for a pre-shift meeting," Pile said.

But what he really thinks will drive the message is storytelling. The 220 managers talk about their experiences at the summit and bring to life the way Alpha lives its culture, appreciates conversations, values its people and envisions its purpose.

EXPERIENCES MAKE THE STORY

Before you have such a critical need to depend on embedded and intentional conversation in your communication plan, get experience in telling stories and making communication personal—beyond the consistent messages of internal media. Company issues change, and so should communication methods. You can gain experience before you may have an urgent need for a different approach.

Now an organizational change communication consultant heading Workwise Communication, Aniko Czinege was managing change communication for a global corporation when it had to reduce expenses, close offices and lay off employees. She had to act quickly to explain to employees what was happening, but the familiar, traditional media communication wasn't the best option in her view. Her solution was personalized communication that was more likely to be trusted by employees whose world was being turned upside down.

"Instead of creating new videos, the company planned a series of team meetings. Rather than hold large conferences, executives scheduled interactive workshops. Newsletters gave way to teleconferences, and information previously disseminated through town hall meetings was shifted to smaller brown bag lunches," Czinege said. "It's all about dialogue and trust."[3]

Czinege had learned the value of conversation from one of her first jobs. She had written a briefing for managers to explain an issue to their employees, and she sat in on one of the meetings to listen to how it went. The manager read the briefing—word for word—to the employees. She heard one of the employees mumble, "Who wrote this rubbish?" What Czinege heard that employee say has influenced her communication planning throughout her career. She includes two-way exchange at every turn so people have a chance to engage in a true discussion about the meaning of a message.

For example, she arranged for a CEO to meet with line managers the night before for dinner or for breakfast the day of a town hall meeting, not just for socializing, but to have a conversation about what's on executives' minds. "Managers have to be supported," she said, just as all employees need to know they have supportive relationships on the job.

She ensures that managers have base knowledge on the topic, a structure for talking with employees and common language to use, including responses to questions employees are likely to ask. In her work in the U.S., U.K., and Europe, she has found that conversation is particularly important for global companies in navigating the cultural differences in business practices.

Once, she encouraged the asking and answering of questions to the extent that she influenced the entire conversation culture at an organization. "We told managers that if you get a question you can't answer, let us know and we will get an answer to you in 24 hours," she said. The unintended but welcomed consequence was this: In knowing they could get an answer if needed, managers were more willing to engage employees in a conversation in the first place—and then discovered they could actually answer most of the questions on their own.

"Managers weren't scared anymore," Czinege said. "We'd created an environment where it was OK to ask questions and have conversations."

Keep in mind:

- There are valid models for communicating differently.
- You have options you may not have considered for communicating about both corporate culture and business strategy.
- No matter what size company you work in, be purposeful when you decide to use conversation, operational communication and media.

Notes

1   T. Pile, personal communication, 2011–2012.

2   Alpha Natural Resources. (n.d.). Your fingerprints are on our future. Retrieved from AlphaNet.

3   A. Czinege, personal communication, 2011.

CHAPTER 8: MAKE COMMUNICATION SMALL

So that's it? Let the CEO talk about business goals and culture while connecting in a personal or emotional way? Expect managers to make sure employees understand how it all relates to their work? Then use mass media to support them and give employees a consistent message?

Yes, you have three proven models for excellent communication:

1. CEO as communicator through two-way conversation about business goals and culture

2. Communication of goals and culture integrated into business operations and processes

3. Consistent messages through internal mass media to improve understanding of strategic goals and culture

It works in theory. The challenge is to apply it in a corporate context when dealing with real people, with all their diversity, complexity, quirks, distractions and preferences.

Audiences for your communication are people, who, by virtue of their employment, have something in common. They are never, however, alike. They have different characteristics, be they geography, training, responsibilities, tenure or others, whether executive or knowledge worker or line staff. Each individual decides what to pay attention to by thinking, "Why should I care?" And if you've captured one person's attention, you can be sure he or she is wondering, "What's in it for me?"

The excellent communication professional sets the stage for conversations to answer those questions. Even when the CEO, manager, or communication professional delivers the information, conversation among work groups and work friends are what drive home the point.

In the next few chapters, we'll look at three natural workplace conversation patterns and how you can add these to your portfolio.

Who's talking	About what?	How to make it excellent?
Supervisor & employee	What this topic means to me, my job or my future	Help managers feel informed so they will own the communication responsibility
Peer opinion leaders	Whether this explanation resonates with me and you	Uncover potential confusion or misunderstanding early and then direct the energy toward positive workplace discussions
Peer to peer	How we support each other to make sense of an ever-changing world	Listen to uncover confusion and refine communication to reinforce supporters

You have already read how managers contribute to excellent communication when conversations are wired in to routine operations, even when there is no employee communication director guiding the discussion. There are additional important and effective ways to embed conversation:

- In a large company where there is a communicator and a plan, topical conversation between a supervisor and an employee can be designed as part of a strategy alongside or independent of communication wired in to operations.

- As another part of the communication strategy, you can develop peer opinion leaders among employees. They converse with a different group than a supervisor's work team, and they can help manage confusion and improve understanding.

- When employees talk among themselves—call it the grapevine or the rumor mill—it has tremendous influence on shared meaning. This is something employee communication directors can include in their communication plans.

We'll look at all three approaches, starting with conversations between supervisors and their employees. Managers spend 75 percent of their time in conversations, according to London Business School professor Donald Sull.[1] Those conversations may happen in formal meetings, phone calls, email exchanges or hallway encounters, so it would seem they have enough practice to excel in two-way dialogue. But not everyone agrees.

SUPERVISOR TO EMPLOYEE

Want to see employee communication directors turn a simple discussion into a verbal smackdown? Mention "manager cascade." At issue is this question: Does supervisor-to-employee communication, especially in the realm of business goals and culture, really work?[2]

Communication directors in large corporations labor to perfect cascading because they know employees like and want face-to-face communication. In a manager cascade, messages move from the top down each level of management until the immediate supervisor talks with each employee. Invariably, the message is garbled by the time it reaches the worker, much like the old parlor game of telephone in which the message is whispered from person to person, and everyone has a good laugh at the difference between the original statement and the ending interpretation.

This is antithetical to the strength of large company employee communication, which is to produce professional media that take a consistent message to the corporate masses. In mid-sized businesses, there are fewer managers, so those managers can hear directly from the CEO exactly what to pass along to employees, but the multiple levels of management in a large business increase the odds of misinterpretation, indifference, and possibly resistance, even when cascading is structured and planned. Managers have to understand the constantly changing strategic information well enough to have conversations with employees and to answer their questions.

> **Managers have to understand the constantly changing strategic information well enough to have conversations with employees and to answer their questions.**

THE CASCADE CLASH

On one side, cascade believers have purposefully surveyed their employees to ask how they want to receive communication. Do they prefer the intranet, an email, even a paper newsletter? Or their supervisor? The usual answer is their supervisor.

When it's done right, through natural conversation, supervisors share what they know in a way that relates to employees as individuals, which makes them feel important.

And why not? When it's done right, through natural conversation, supervisors share what they know in a way that relates to employees as individuals, which makes them feel important. And employees can ask questions for further clarification about how the topic affects them, their job, their family or their future.

And employees can ask questions for further clarification about how the topic affects them, their job, their family or their future.

On the other side, corporate communication directors have battle scars to prove that when you rely on dozens or thousands of managers to deliver a message, it fails somewhere and often. CEOs feel the pain too, one reason executives are motivated to depend on communicators who can get their words directly to employees. On matters as critical as business goals and culture, why not skip over the middleman? That has its own problems, though, because managers will always need to be in the loop to answer employees' questions about how their work contributes to corporate goals, and to model and reward the right actions and attitudes.

The cascade skeptics have survey research on their side, too. When a questionnaire asks employees how they want to receive information *about a specific topic*, the answer is "my supervisor" only some of the time, mostly when the topic raises questions about how they and their jobs might be affected. Otherwise, employees recognize that some topics are best delivered other ways. A comprehensive list of products, wide-ranging competitive information, global financial updates, or general corporate announcements are easier to communicate online or in a newsletter.

And how do supervisors feel about their role in a cascade? Being the source of knowledge reinforces their role in the chain of command, and that can feel good. Having a manager who is close to the action and willing to share gives comfort to employees. But the truth is that when it comes to talking about corporate strategy or culture, many results-oriented supervisors question whether it is really their job to take time to discuss anything they perceive as less pressing than meeting with customers or meeting their numbers. And they certainly don't have time to take another communication skills training course.

Mostly, though, managers are scared.

Supervisors often do not want to talk with their teams about the details of business goals or issues because they do not "feel smart" about corporate topics. This can be especially true of managers who are separated from headquarters and therefore, even unintentionally, out of the loop. Though they may be autonomous in running small offices, that fear and separation make these managers quite different from small-business CEOs leading a similar sized group of employees. Recall that in excellent micro-businesses, CEOs with no training or professionally prepared communication tools are confident that they can effectively explain business goals to employees. What if the dutiful supervisor delivers a presentation sent from headquarters, and an employee asks for clarification on a particular point that the manager can't answer?

Recognize what is happening. A communication team back at headquarters put its best effort into explaining the issue with bullet-point slides for supervisors to use, maybe because that is how ideas spread at headquarters. In the plant or store or branch office, people don't expect to sit around a conference room looking at a deck of slides with corporate jargon. This is communication? No wonder people are asking, what does this mean? Who wrote this?

MANAGERS AS THE WELLSPRING

Like a giant waterfall, cascading information from the top can be impressive. In small communication, though, a wellspring of information close to the working team ripples out in a similarly powerful way.

Supervisors are a critical link. "The line manager is a continuous improvement leader. In this role they need to paint a clear vision, model the way, provide information and resources while focusing on improving the relevant numbers—the financial, people and operating numbers," said Jim Shaffer, a consultant who specializes in operational communication.[3]

This is especially true of managers in small, separated offices of large companies. In many ways, communication and conversation at each isolated location are like those in a small business. For employees in separated offices, the manager is the center of their universe, just as the CEO is the center of the communication universe for employees in micro-businesses.

An employee communication director can rescue small-office managers, even when they do not necessarily think they need help with communication skills. Small-office managers spend much of their day in face-to-face encounters anyway. It makes sense to include tactics in your formal communication program that provide small-office managers with business information and ideas for making corporate goals and culture relevant to work teams.

SEED THEIR CONVERSATIONS

Managers want their employees to take them seriously, of course, even if they don't quite know how communication makes that happen. Instead of training site managers and line supervisors to parrot corporate goals, offer ideas that seed conversations. Give them stories to repeat that send a message they are more comfortable with: understanding how their own office can contribute to the company's success. You might even offer tips for building storytelling into regular conversations.

> **Tip:** Pick up where HR leaves off. Human resources or organizational development professionals often address the performance dialogue between a supervisor and a worker.
>
> Corporate executives know that regular interactions between worker and supervisor have a tremendous effect on job satisfaction and career progression—both of which ultimately affect a company's excellence. But so does shared meaning around goals and culture that emerges through conversations.
>
> Any supervisor-employee dialogue related to reporting or coaching may fall outside your employee communication responsibility. What about supervisor-employee discussions on corporate goals and culture? Make those supervisor-employee conversations part of your formal communication plan.

"From a leader's perspective, it's going from being a teller to being a storyteller, being the one who can create meaning for people so that many people can make decisions. Instead of saying, hey, you do this, and you do that, we should come back and say, this is what's going on for our organization," said Nilofer Merchant,[4] author of *The New How: Creating business solutions through collaborative strategy*. A story sets the stage, defines the challenge and moves to resolution. "What's going on—that's a story to tell! Here's what our context is. And here's what we face. And here's what we think is important. What do you think?"

⭐ Paul Smith had a compelling story to tell when he led a team at a large paper products business that was charged with developing a long-term strategy—so far out in the future that some of the people might be retired before the first new product was introduced. He wanted to inspire and motivate the team, build commitment and courage, and show them that what seemed impossible was important.[5]

Smith wove the tale of a similar business that started in 1865 in Finland. It began as a pulp mill and then started making paper. He described how in those days, paper had essentially two uses: newsprint and stationery for writing letters. Those were the two primary forms of communication back then, so the paper company was essentially in the communication business, and it had cornered its market. So what came next?

The company in his story started acquiring other companies, like a rubber manufacturing plant, which led to buying a copper cable manufacturer—a good investment with the spread of the telegraph. This paper-maker was following a communications industry path. Acquisition aft er acquisition placed that pulp mill among the best-known brands, and it is still alive today. The company in question—Nokia.

"I told that story to my guys in the paper business," Smith said in a video on his website, leadwithastory.com, going on to explain to the team, "I'm not suggesting we decide how we are going to make cellphones.

"The point is that we get to either decide how we are going to expand into the future and how to make a choiceful business," he told them, "or we can let it happen randomly—or it can not happen at all."[6]

He created meaning and set the stage for the challenge ahead. "The story can help people understand that, yeah, that is achievable, because somebody else did it," Smith said.

A powerful story like that deserves retelling in other settings as well. A plugged-in employee communication director can uncover such storytelling as it happens and then plant those stories as seeds in other business conversations. Smith's particular story had power in energizing that one team. Retold in other settings, the story could improve understanding in other business units about what's going on around the company. In this case, managers whose departments interact with the paper products area could retell the story to start dialogue about overall company goals.

Like stories, questions engage people. As an employee communication director, you can provide managers with questions to ask their employees that are related to the issue up for discussion. Once you explain what's going on so managers feel comfortable with the topic, you can encourage them to use conversation-starter questions:

- Why should we care about this in our department?
- What will it mean for the work we do?
- What actions do we need to take to achieve the goals?
- What milestones can we measure along the way to stay on track?

It's probably a good idea to offer a couple of possible answers for managers to keep in their back pockets to use until employees will feel comfortable diving into the dialogue. For example, to the question, "Why should we care about this in our department?" you might provide guidance along the line of, "We can keep our customers from being lured away by the competition." Seed the questions, and seed some answers. It is, simply, a conversational way of presenting your key messages so that people see the relevance to themselves.

Whether providing a repeatable story to managers or questions for them to bring up in a dialogue, there are two audiences: the ultimate employee-receiver plus the intermediate bearer of the message to a distinct group.

The two-way communication model for symmetrical communication expands to incorporate the supervisor

Communicator   Supervisor   Work team

That's right. Communicate with company managers, separately. The more they absorb about corporate goals and culture that relate to the work they do, the smarter they will feel when they actually do have conversations with their staff. Then they just might have a confident response when they are asked to clarify a corporate issue.

"Might" is the operative word. Just because you help managers in your company better understand corporate goals and culture doesn't lead them directly to having conversations about these things with employees. As the employee communication director, you are asking them to do something new and different that, to some degree, would cause anxiety for anyone. You can turn "might" into "will" by helping managers change their own behavior and feel comfortable talking with their staff.

WHAT'S IN IT FOR ME, THE SUPERVISOR?

Stanford professor BJ Fogg has defined three elements needed to change behavior: motivation, ability and trigger.[7] The trio work for all kinds of communication efforts, and you can address all three when you involve managers themselves in a conversation about their role in talking to employees. Here are some examples of what you can do:

1. **Motivation.** Ask your managers, "What difference will it make if you engage your staff in a conversation about the specific issue at hand?" Managers might answer that progress toward a goal will be less painful for the whole team, or they can have influence over the outcome, or they'll be recognized for success, for instance.

2. **Ability.** You want to make things easy. Because ability can have more to do with ease than talent, you can provide a simple Q&A document so managers have answers to questions they are likely to be asked by employees. That will enhance their ability.

3. **Trigger.** Soon after you give managers their challenge to communicate about a particular topic, deliver a consistent message to employees, guiding them to find out how the topic affects their department by asking their manager. That will prompt managers to step up.

When supervisors are clear about corporate goals and culture and build these into conversations as their regular routine, they fulfill a huge communication role. Remember that companies survive and thrive when employees feel connected to their work, and that happens when they have information about how their work fits in and furthers business goals.

Like the CEO who knows her employees well and embodies the goals and culture of her micro-business, the best supervisors help their employees connect the dots between the work they do each day and the overall achievement of business goals.

The other factor that employees need to feel connected to their work is supportive relationships on the job. Conversations and storytelling engender an emotional connection, open communication, and trust that reinforce both culture and support. Supervisors don't carry this responsibility alone. Peers offer a support network, which we will explore in the next two chapters.

PERSONAL CHANGE

But first, one more point. When you, as the employee communication director, encourage managers to have conversations with employees about culture and big-picture goals, steer clear of committing asymmetrical communication yourself—persuading line managers to communicate with their employees. Understand that managers may be unwilling, and not only because they may not feel informed about the topic. They also know as well as anyone that open, honest conversations with employees can open the door to unpredictable situations. It's frightening to know that as they listen to employees, managers may hear something that leads them to personally take a different stand than they expected.

"They have to be comfortable with the fact that they aren't trying to change people but that actually they may change themselves when they enter this kind of relationship with people," said Ryan Williams, a partner with Tekara Organizational Effectiveness in Toronto. Williams stressed that leaders must be open to changing themselves based on the listening they do. "It isn't a relationship where you're only seeking to influence one way. This has big implications," he explained.[8]

Williams calls it transformational leadership, not a transactional exchange of words. His research shows that transformational leadership works best in a "clan" culture and in "innovative" companies—again, excellent management comes first, and small communication carries the message of culture in clan or community conversations.

Like everyone else, line managers want to know how they, personally, can link their work to business goals and enjoy the advantage of a supporting culture—and that taking time for conversations about culture and goals with their employees is one path. They want to know they have support when they do so. They need to be prepared for the messy and difficult conversations that may arise. You might set up a forum for managers to share their experiences when having these conversations with their work groups. Let line managers learn from each other about how their own leadership style has deeper meaning when they transform rather than transact communication. And it gives you a chance to listen to managers, completing the symmetrical communication loop.

Here is what we've learned about communication and front-line managers:

- Employees depend on managers to let them know how their work fits in and furthers business goals and to support them in doing their work.

- Front-line managers are, as would be expected, reluctant to answer questions about corporate goals they don't understand well themselves. Employee communication directors can help them be in the know and help them recognize their important role in shaping shared meaning.

- For those two reasons, managers are a critical audience in any employee communication plan, not to become human megaphones in cascading communication, but to be storytellers to relate goals and culture to their teams—and to fellow managers.

Notes

1   Sull, D. (2010, March). Are you ready to rebound? *Harvard Business Review*, 71–74.

2   Sinickas, A. (1992, November). Supervisors are not the preferred communicators! *IABC Communication World*. Retrieved from http://www.sinicom.com/Sub%20Pages/pubs/articles/article28.htm

3   Shaffer, J. (2004, July 1). Measureable payoff. *Communication World,* 20(4), 22–23.

4   Merchant, N. (2010, April 26). Real collaboration. AMA Edgewise. Podcast. Retrieved from http://www.amanet.org/training/podcasts/3666.aspx

5   Smith, P. (n.d.). Why tell stories? [video]. Retrieved from http://www.leadwithastory.com/more-video/keynote-videos/

6   Smith.

7   Fogg, BJ. (n.d.). *BJ Fogg's Behavior Model*. Retrieved from http://www.behaviormodel.org/

8   Williams, R., & Holtz, S. (2010, July 15). FIR book review: Open Leadership by Charlene Li. For Immediate Release Podcast. Retrieved from http://www.forimmediaterelease.biz/index.php?/weblog/comments/fir_book_review_open_leadership_by_charlene_li/

CHAPTER 9: GUIDE CONVERSATIONS THAT RESONATE

There *are* natural communicators out there.

These people ask questions around the office even when others might be embarrassed or too reserved to do so (not that there's anything wrong with that). Forthright questioners want to hear the whole story so they understand what affects them or what they need to act on—that's the way their minds work—then they impart the new information to people they know.

When their curiosity and willingness to share what they know are combined with an ability to talk about things in a way that is personal and relevant to friends, you've got yourself a peer opinion leader. Peer opinion leaders are seldom supervisors with any authority over a distinct group of employees, but they do influence the people around them. They tailor their messages to their friends and co-workers in ways that can clarify expected behavior.

Lucky for you, they love to be "in the know." People like this are perfect partners in excellent communication. Find them. Enlist them.

People who love to be "in the know" are perfect partners in excellent communication. Find them. Enlist them.

This could seem counterintuitive, even frightening, to you. Employee communication directors have studied and mastered their skills to deliver the best message at the right time for measurable results. We even coach executives and train managers to be better communicators. And now we're supposed to give such an important communication role to random people in the workforce? It is humbling to think that opinion leaders can do so much to achieve excellent employee communication for our companies.

But what a partnership it can be. These people are, of course, already having conversations that resonate in the workplace. You're not giving away control. You never had it. You can either be frightened or incented to harness that reality. What you do have is influence. What you *do* know is how to create the best message; give it to peer opinion leaders to share in their own, effective style.

First, talk with them as you begin a communication initiative, so you will hear any potential objections or disagreements with your messages. By practicing two-way, open communication at this level, opinion leaders can help you manage conflict or confusion while improving understanding—the essence of excellent communication.

⭐ At Engelhard Corp., the employee communication director asked heads of departments who the natural leaders were and networked them. Regular email and phone calls jumpstarted the dialogue and offered a way for them to share knowledge with each other. At the same time, the director made sure they knew how they could serve as communication ambassadors.[1]

Setting communication strategy and managing communication media and content have traditionally been ways to view the role of an employee communicator. Influencing conversation is a further role—embedding important messages into discussions people are already having about work.

WHAT IT IS: EMBEDDED CONVERSATION

An untapped opportunity for many large companies is embedding conversation in work groups through peer opinion leaders, not managers. A manager remains a top choice to help employees understand how their work fits in and furthers business goals. A peer opinion leader is particularly helpful when the topic relates to group expectations or cultural behavior needed to achieve goals even when no one else is looking. Resourceful employee communication directors at large companies can partner with peer opinion leaders to describe behavior and give reasons for "the way we do things around here" as they discuss current topics. Actually living the values is more important than talking about them, of course. Still, people need to hear words and phrases that capture the essence of those values to repeat and explicitly pass them on—much like a one-year-old child may recognize objects but, without a vocabulary, cannot speak about them. Shared language is part of shared understanding.

Peer opinion leaders do their communicating over lunch, at team meetings, in a carpool, on blogs or wherever their lives take them. They plant ideas that are relevant to a particular individual or group into a face-to-face conversation or on Facebook, not something mass media can do well. "There's more to be gained by getting 20 people to listen to each other than by sending out 5,000 newsletters or videos," according to consultant Jim Shaffer.[2]

⭐ At a brand-name manufacturing, products and media company, employees who had been with the company for 20 years or more, but not in any management role, were invited annually to the headquarters for group discussion. Executives talked about the company and listened to ideas from the invited employees, who had long-term connections to co-workers. That's another example of how to seek out peer opinion leaders.

People who haven't been promoted to management but have developed friendships are a good choice, according to Mike Ward, partner at The Brand Inside in London. "Opinion leaders are often popular because they're funny, charismatic, passionate and articulate. So they exhibit a lot of what one would like to see in a leader. Why aren't they formal leaders? Often because they're not prepared to play politics or work long hours," Ward said. "They often prefer to be an informal leader rather than become a formal one."[3]

When peer opinion leaders propel information, the model is a two-step flow of communication similar to the two-step flow with managers (chapter 8). In the first step, a message and feedback move between the communication director and an opinion leader. In the second step, the opinion leader exchanges information with others. Then, the opinion leader has more feedback for the communicator to complete the loop.

The two-way communication model for symmetrical communication also expands to incorporate peer opinion leaders

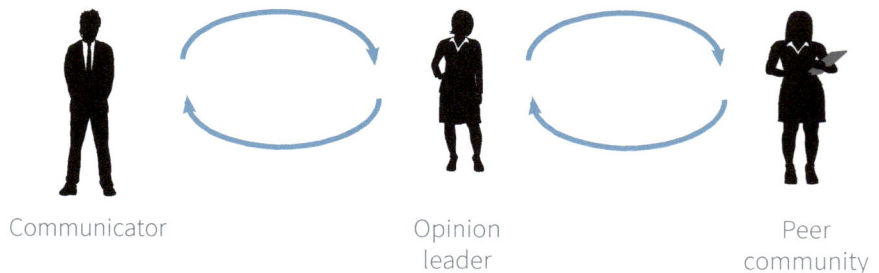

Communicator   Opinion leader   Peer community

By engaging peer opinion leaders in dialogue at the first step, they become involved in managing confusion or conflict and improving understanding at that point and the next. They are the symmetrical communicators out there, and you can hear, through them, what employees are saying or how they are reacting to your message.

> **They are the symmetrical communicators out there, and you can hear, through them, what employees are saying or how they are reacting to your message.**

When you take on the role of listening to peer opinion leaders and to the feedback they bring from others, be prepared to adjust your message to make it clearer—or even change the tone or intent as you come to understand any resistance or concern employees have.

WHY IT WORKS: INFORMATION MOVES FAST

To understand how opinion leaders actually contribute to excellent communication, we may need to change the commonly used phrase "peer opinion leader" to a better descriptor, "opinion broker." These people are not so much on top or leading anything, according to Ronald S. Burt, author of *The Social Capital of Opinion Leaders*, "as at the edge of things, not leaders within groups so much as brokers between groups."[4] Because opinion brokers are not supervisors with authority over a defined organizational structure, the communities of workers they influence are fluid and overlapping, not necessarily defined by function within a company or geographic location or even time zone. Opinion brokers are well-connected people who span gaps between one community and another in a network of communities.

"Opinion brokers now identified as network entrepreneurs…monitor information more effectively than bureaucratic control. They move information faster, and to more people [and] can tailor solutions to the specific individuals…replacing the boiler-plate solutions of formal bureaucracy," Burt wrote.[5] He reported that this tailored solution gives peer opinion leaders their influence over people, leading co-workers to adopt the attitudes or actions that the new information seeks to effect. A converted co-worker then convinces another co-worker, and the "*new* way we do things around here" becomes contagious.

> **A converted co-worker then convinces another co-worker, and the "new way we do things around here" becomes contagious.**

Peer opinion leaders are always talking and tailoring the conversation to what they know will resonate with different groups. Influence like that needs to be encouraged and guided, not repressed. You have a chance to embed a guided conversation in work groups through opinion leaders, not only through managers. It's a positive way to bring the grapevine or rumor mill into the communication strategy.

This is the author's social graph on LinkedIn, with the author at the center and connected to individuals all around, bridging community clusters of different colors. The screen shot is low resolution.

© 2014 LinkedIn

WHO THEY ARE: FINDING INFLUENCERS IN YOUR COMPANY

Of course, the first step is to figure out how to identify your organization's peer opinion leaders and their reach across different communities. Social network graphs show the online relationships between people by digitally mapping community nodes. Peer opinion leaders might have more connections, and opinion brokers are likely to be connectors between multiple communities. In either case, peers turn to them for their knowledge and the way they help make sense of what is happening.

⭐ Think like a small company and just pick some people. It's inexpensive and relatively simple, and it's working for Eric Haman, corporate communications manager at The Clemens Family Corp., a large meat products company based in Pennsylvania. Reaching more than 2,000 employees by media is difficult there because most do not work at computers, and more than half speak languages other than English, including Arabic, Spanish and Vietnamese. Embedding messages in workplace conversation—by native speakers—was a viable and logical method to transcend different languages and customs.

Haman said identifying influencers was fairly easy. He looked for people who seemed to be in the know, vocal and engaged. "If we are having a group meeting, they are the ones who attend and ask questions," Haman explained.[6] He looked around and asked others, department by department, to find people who seemed to fit the bill. He designated about 100 influencers, ensuring that each area was represented. If you're doing the mental math, the influencer to employee ratio is 1 to 20—the micro-business size for communication strength in conversations.

Though he would like to bring this group together regularly for face-to-face meetings, most are hourly employees working on production lines in various facilities. So Haman travels to the production facilities to meet with his team of peer opinion leaders on their home turf. "I don't want to create a burden by pulling people off the line. Once we meet with them, they can go right back and start spreading the word," he said.

WHAT THEY DO WELL: REVERSE THE CASCADE

Haman values his peer opinion leaders for their ability to make the water flow upward, if you will, instead of receiving information and cascading it down, as managers might be asked to do.

"I don't say, 'Here's a new policy, now go and spread the word.' Instead, I ask, 'What are you hearing? Or what are some ways we can improve?'" In other words, he asks them to communicate with him, too, and he listens. In listening, it's important to have the ability and willingness to react. "If we start hearing stuff and nothing is done, influencers will start to question whether they should say anything to me at all," he said. That is all consistent with the upside-down evidence of two-way excellent communication from Chapter 1:

- Excellent management comes first, so that excellent employee communication can be integrated into the daily operations of excellent corporations.
- Excellent management is willing to enter into challenging conversations with employees about complex and life-changing workplace issues.

> **Tip:** Your employees will consider different peer opinion leaders to be more credible on some topics than others. One person may be a peer opinion leader on Topic A for Community Y, while a different person is a better influencer on Topic B in Community Z.
>
> Popular online scoring algorithms aim to identify people with clout or credibility in social media, but be aware of the limitations of automated authority scores. Recognize inherent deficiencies in social media analytics in identifying the **topics** around which certain influencers have clout or credibility as well as the different **groups** over which they have influence. Common scoring tools may only count the extent of someone's **reach** or generosity in sharing knowledge or information.

Haman describes one such unpleasant conversation with peer opinion leaders when the turbulent economy kept the company from paying employees a bonus based on profitability. "The perception was that this bonus program was going away," Haman said. That could easily have resulted in less engagement in achieving shared goals. Instead, without spending money on media or launching an engagement campaign, he simply explained to the influencers what was really happening. He was able to seed workplace conversations through the peer opinion leaders by telling them that the bonus program was not going away, and, in fact, the company hoped for a financial turnaround so it could pay out on that bonus program after the next business cycle.

"When employees hear their fellow employees saying that this particular payoff is not going to take place but hopefully the next one will, it's real to them," Haman said.

Making it real is what peer opinion leaders can do.

⭐ When company executives listen to peer opinion leaders, what may seem minor or even invisible at the top comes into plain view. Mike Ward tells the story of one of his clients that created a steering group to clear blockages facing its champions—the peer opinion leaders. "The champions fed back an ongoing gripe about the condition of the workforces' uniforms and that this was hindering their pride in the organization," Ward said. "The steering group ordered new uniforms, and this symbolic barrier was removed. It had been a real distraction and hindered the implementation of a program that sought to align employee behavior with the external brand promise."

When you engage in balanced, symmetrical communication like this, you will find things you as a communicator or executive need to do differently or better. To help avoid unnecessary messiness and disruption, Ward suggests making sure middle managers understand the business benefit of peer opinion leaders. "They may be mavericks; they may be disruptive," he said, which may be a subconscious response to defuse any image of being a tool of management. In fact, Ward recommends finding the people managers may see as mavericks or dissidents, who at the same time are passionate about the company and already exhibit the "right" behaviors. "Inspire and equip them to spread the word to the peers," Ward said. "It's a slog to get going, but it's highly cost-effective and is sustainable long-term."

"There's nothing that carries the message into every corner of the organization like word of mouth," Ward said.

Try the following with employee influencers:

- Peer opinion leaders seek out information, and they eagerly share it. You can provide peer opinion leaders correct, up-to-date knowledge. Eager to show what they know, they will tailor their new knowledge into relevant workplace conversations based on what their friends and co-workers find interesting.

- Savvy employee communication directors enlist peer opinion leaders before delivering new messages or topics, because opinion leaders can point out what will and won't resonate with other employees. This helps manage potential confusion or conflict to improve understanding—the essence of excellent communication.

- Give peer opinion leaders more than mere facts to repeat. They want to know the "whys." Peer opinion leaders excel in passing along culture messages by painting a picture of desired behavior and giving reasons for "the way we do things around here."

Notes

1   K. Kelly, personal communication, 2003.

2   Shaffer, J. (2006). High value, Low cost rules! One Fellow's lessons, Jim Shaffer Group [PowerPoint]. Retrieved from http://www.iabc.com/education/pdf/JimShaffer_TerrySimpson_M16.pdf

3   M. Ward, personal communication, 2011.

4   Burt, R. (1999). *The social capital of opinion leaders*. p. 1. Retrieved from http://faculty.chicagobooth.edu/ronald.burt/research/files/SCOL.pdf

5   Burt, pp. 15–16.

6   E. Haman, personal communication, 2003.

CHAPTER 10: GIVE A VOICE TO SUPPORTERS

With the prospect of seeding conversations between managers and their employees, and those between peer influencers and their co-workers, you might dream of gaining control over conversations at the workplace.

Don't.

Let's look more deeply at peer-to-peer conversation within communities—or tribes, to use a trendy term with anthropologic roots—that develop within the workplace.

EMPLOYEES BOND IN COMMUNITIES

People with common interests form a community even without physical proximity. Because adults spend a third of their lives at work, communities on the job arise naturally—but not necessarily because the members have adjacent cubicles.

Employees find co-workers with common interests and become friends despite departmental lines. Communities form without regard for bureaucratic compartmentalization and defy organizational charts. They may seem to be without order, but in fact, companies flourish with healthy communities. Employees bonded in communities learn faster, perform better and are more committed to the company. Co-workers in a community find motivation and meaning in their work through shared goals.

See if this applies in your job. When you have a question, you call on others in the workplace (not necessarily supervisors or even co-workers in the same department), who will most likely know the answer to your question. Though you may not consciously consider this "community," you turn to people who have certain experience or knowledge, and you feel comfortable enough to ask them for their advice—and then to follow their guidance.

While communities defy physical boundaries, they do impose boundaries on members.

While communities defy physical boundaries, they do impose boundaries on members. A community shares an understanding of—and expects—appropriate

> **Community and Communication**
>
> Traditional definitions of community round up all the people within certain boundaries. The *American Heritage Dictionary*, for example, defines a community as "a group of people living in the same locality and under the same government." These days, this Middle English-era word has thrown off the shackles of physical boundaries. An online community attracts people from around the world to exchange messages on a topic of mutual interest. People with common interests form a community even without physical proximity.
>
> A community defined by shared interests instead of shared location actually comes closer to the etymology of the word. Community comes from the Latin *communis*, meaning common. Another English word, communication, comes from the same Latin root and suggests nuance to the concept of community. To communicate, again according to American Heritage, means "to have an interchange, as of ideas," "to express oneself in such a way that one is readily and clearly understood," and even "to be connected." This linguistic similarity is seen in other world languages as well.

behavior. Employees in a community expose inappropriate behavior. According to Alex Filip, deputy director, office of communications for the U.S. Consumer Product Safety Commission, a community's value increases during times of change or when facing difficult tasks: "If people are challenged, they either measure up or their community helps so they do not fail."[1]

At work, social boundaries affect everything from quality to ethics. If a community makes it clear that unnecessary absenteeism strains the people who have to pick up the slack, community members will show up daily. If the community holds fast to honesty and frowns on padded expense reports, people who break this unwritten rule will be excluded.

In his role as a consultant with The Brand Inside, Mike Ward said his conversations with client company employees illustrate the power of positive peer influence on behavior. Typical conversations go something like this:[2]

Recall the employee numbers categories that provide guidance for communication strengths based on company size:

Large business
More than 500 employees

Mid-sized business
Up to 500 employees

Micro business
Up to 20 employees

"Does your boss see everything you do?"

"No."

"Do your peers see everything you do?"

"Pretty much."

"And do you listen to your boss when he or she gives you guidance on your behavior?"

"No. In fact I often resent it and may do the opposite just for the hell of it."

"So do you listen to your peers?"

"I guess so. They're doing the same job, and they're normally just trying to help rather than passing on orders."

"So who is a more effective behavioral guide: boss or peer?"

"Peer."

Peers who share the meaning of their work create behavioral consistency—reason enough for company executives to accept and even nurture workplace communities. But nurture doesn't mean force. It's not a new way to control workers' actions or attitudes, primarily because communities fall outside managers' span of control. Communities are not the same as imposed work teams, which are formed as a corporate solution for accountability and for assigning resources.

Of course, a defined work team could turn into a community whose members share an understanding of work issues and develop friendships over time. Usually, communities are constantly evolving, regardless of team assignments. They do not necessarily have face-to-face interactions, either. Digital natives—who grew up friending and following peers in social media—can navigate a fluid network for guidance and advice. Robert Wendover, director of the Center for Generational Studies, suggests these employees need their smartphones on the job, because accessing their trusted networks is the best way they know to solve a problem or answer an immediate question.[3] Online collaboration builds this digital experience and expectation into ongoing conversations about goals and culture.

HOW MANY PEOPLE DOES IT TAKE TO HAVE A CONVERSATION?

How many distinct and opinionated individuals can truly bond into a trusting community, to exchange ideas and reach a common understanding—in a workplace or any place? Politicians and celebrities try to build their online social networks into the tens of thousands, sometimes into the millions. Isn't that just a giant mass-media mailing list—not a group of friends? It seems to corrupt the concepts of both "social" and "network."

Malcolm Gladwell's popular book, *The Tipping Point*, reviews biological and sociological reasons why a manageable group size for conversing about common interests stops at 150 people,[4] well within the mid-sized company category or even a department within a large company.

While an individual may depend on 150 acquaintances for insight into matters of common interest, close friendships with 10 or 12 people bring the ideal community size down even further—similar to the micro-business category. British scientist Robin Dunbar calls these smaller communities "sympathy groups."[5] The members know each other personally, converse regularly about common interests, and share information in a personal, practical and memorable way—all factors that more clearly define a community than people just living in the same village. It also sounds a lot like the hoped-for communication in businesses—connections that provide support at work and link personal contributions to organizational goals.

BONDED WITHOUT FENCES

Dunbar's science reveals that our brains predispose us to relate with groups of certain size. Where communication plays a role is in reaching a tipping point through smaller communities within the employee audience.

In any organization, you'll find supporters of goals and culture at one end of a bell curve and detractors at the other end. The vast middle or statistically average group can be pulled down the slope in either direction. They may get off the fence to join one side or the other, depending on who is louder and more believable, the supporters or the detractors. Employee communication directors have the ammunition the supporters need to be both credible and resonant.

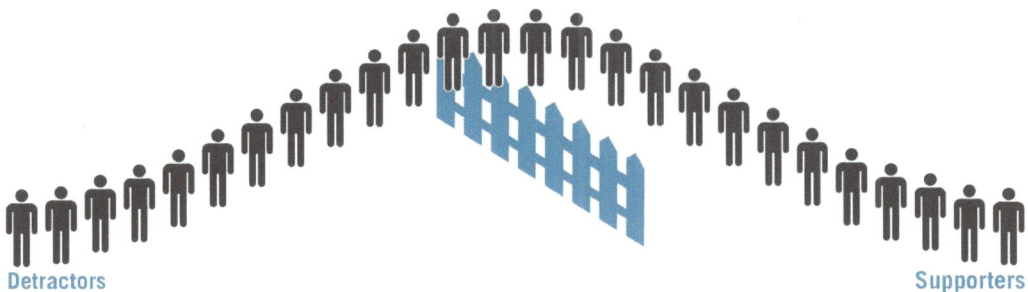

Detractors　　　　　　　　　　　　　　　　　　　　　　　**Supporters**

Clarify issues for the detractors and give creditbility to supporters for their peer-to-peer conversations; you may see the majority of employees get off the fence of indifference because of their new understanding.

It doesn't take much. Only 10 percent of employees—or any group—need to be fully committed to an idea for that idea to become adopted by the majority, according to scientists at Rensselaer Polytechnic Institute. Using computer modeling and analytical methods, they discovered the 10-percent tipping point for the minority opinion to become a majority belief. In the computer models, it didn't matter whether people were directly connected to each other or linked to an opinion leader and open to that person's views.

It works, because "people do not like to hold an unpopular opinion and are always seeking to try locally to come to consensus," according to one of the researchers, Sameet Sreenivasan. "As agents of change start to convince more and more people, the situation begins to change."[6]

With such a small percentage required to spread opinions, it becomes imperative for employee communication directors to make peer conversation not only a priority but also a continuing effort in their strategic plan. Employee communication directors can reinforce the supporters and address the issues raised by the detractors.

Often, detractors are merely misinformed, and fence sitters don't have enough information to become supporters. Together, they make up a huge portion of the workforce. "Over time, research has shown that three quarters of companies have more detractors on staff than advocates," said James Garrick of Insync Surveys in Melbourne. "This is a major challenge and missed opportunity."[7]

Information is on your side, and understanding follows. In some ways, excellent communication—improving understanding and avoiding confusion—is at its purest at the peer-to-peer level.

"Keep your friends close, and your enemies closer" was the advice of the ancient Chinese military general Sun-Tzu. Detractors don't consider themselves our enemies, nor should we, yet there is value in keeping them close to information. Good people come to opposing conclusions when they don't have sufficient information or when they feel like their personal situations are ignored as decisions are being made. When detractors are invited by an employee communication director to be part of a peer opinion team, they have a chance to talk through any misunderstandings. In raising their concerns, detractors guide communicators in adjusting the plan or the message to make it realistic and appreciated by a larger employee base. Those dissenters can become supporters and push others right over the fence onto the supporter side—good reason to enter into conversations with the people who vocally disagree. "Managers dislike such people but we love them," Mike Ward said. "Ninety-five percent make great champions and bring other dissenters."

TAP THE GRAPEVINE

To get better at giving a voice to supporters and knowing what to say to detractors and fence sitters, you just need to listen. You can manage the temptation to manage tribes by setting out to understand how workplace communities hash out meaning and relevancy in the first place. People chat about the official line and whether it matches their experiences on the job. All along, they are influenced by their community—the people they trust.

Despite being a significant part of the communication landscape, community conversation—gossip, the grapevine or the rumor mill—might seem outside the purview of employee communication professionals and is probably denigrated by management. Executives may be inclined to ignore communities or consider them troublesome cliques that gossip.

The grapevine has escaped being directly managed in most companies. According to research led by Suzanne Crampton, who is on the faculty at Grand Valley State University in Michigan, 92 percent of organizations had no policy to deal with the grapevine. In fact, many business observers actually dissuade management from even trying to control the grapevine.[8]

Tracking gossip doesn't mean you can or even want to control it; however, you should listen. The *Public Personnel Management* report identified these grapevine factors that reveal reasons for building communication strategies around grapevine chatter:[9]

- The chatting uncovers subjects that are important to employees and reveals the intensity of their interest in these subjects.
- The chatting reveals topics that employees find ambiguous or unclear, ones that may need more formal communication.
- The chatting signals the health—or perceived instability—of the working environment and reveals true levels of trust in management.

Think of the helpful insight that can come from knowing which subjects are important to employees and their level of interest in them, which topics they find ambiguous or unclear, and how much they trust management. Dunbar saw gossip-spreading in a positive light too, as a way communities establish and keep track of relationships. Communicators can use this intelligence to address conflict and improve understanding if they grasp the grapevine's role in building a support network and in giving meaning to people's jobs.

Gossip grows from a kernel of truth, but some points are exaggerated precisely because the community considers them important. Other points are ignored as irrelevant. Astute employee communication directors recognize gossip as the story that makes sense to the people spreading it. Listening to how people react or in which direction they take the facts can help communicators respond so that they can reduce confusion and improve understanding. Knowing how people augment that kernel of truth keeps executives from overlooking the unintended consequences of a corporate action or decision.

"Those who are able to understand the power of the grapevine will be better prepared to utilize it to provide stability and credibility in the work environment that is needed in order to achieve organizational goals," said Jitendra Mishra, also a faculty member at Grand Valley State University.[10]

These conversations about work, personal or virtual, ultimately help people make sense of what is happening in their company to reach a common understanding. That makes them a community—and helps them establish supportive relationships on the job along with knowing how their work furthers business goals.

CULTURE FROM DAY ONE

Making sense of work starts the first day on the job, as a new employee begins adjusting to the company. Typically, the employee signs benefits or tax documents and hears an unblemished picture of the company during a formal orientation.

Next, the supervisor explains job procedures and expectations, with visions of this newcomer becoming a model employee as a perfect representation of the corporate culture in the race to the company's goals.

But then, the ideal and real blend as co-workers explain the actual situation through their eyes. Which part of the dress code is truly enforced? What does the boss really expect when he or she asks you to work late? Why do we like working here? What gets measured and what can slip? Fellow employees tell stories about how the boss thinks, things that have happened to co-workers or how the company deals with certain situations. Culture is passed along.

As each new person arrives, colleagues get another chance to talk about how they think and act, and as they teach and reach for words to explain the culture, they understand even better themselves. The new person asks more questions, and in the give and take of the conversations, this community arrives at a common meaning for what goes on at work.

This shared understanding also happens to be the essence of excellent employee communication conversations. As these conversations orient people, they become immensely important when you consider that all employees—not just new hires—arrive as newcomers at the same-but-changing company where they may have worked for years, even decades.

> ## All employees—not just new hires—arrive as newcomers at the same-but-changing company where they may have worked for years, even decades.

THE SAME COMPANY IS DIFFERENT TODAY

Acculturation happens not only to new hires but also to all employees. They may not go through a traditional orientation program again, but they face new goals and the expectation of doing things in innovative ways, with a heightened need to know how their jobs contribute to company success. The culture and mission may endure while the day-to-day work pivots. Marketplace pressures reshape old companies into new ones through restructuring or redefined missions practically overnight. Employees find themselves labeled brand ambassadors for new products and services sold to different consumers in an unfamiliar global competition.

As an employee communication director developing a communication plan about yet another change, you can look beyond internal media, appreciating the value of peer-to-peer conversation in uniting employees in relationships to achieve goals. What sparks that conversation?

Growth, for sure—as with BeCore, a small-sized events agency for some of the largest brands in the world, and with the technology giant Juniper Networks. In part, their respective examples reflect different sizes and company complexity. In both cases, though, the patterns are the same: Encourage conversations that solidify the culture around the company mission and values.

⭐ BeCore, an experiential marketing agency in Los Angeles, was growing so fast that it needed a new building with space for its 30 employees. "Our culture was almost in-your-face when it was our small executive board and four or five project managers all working in the same room together at our old office," recalled Whitney Long, account manager.[11]

"In our shiny new office, with more levels, walls and doors, it didn't take long for our colorful group of people to notice and feel the difference even our physical distance was making—not to mention the pace at which everyone was moving. It became obvious, then, that we would need to make an effort at maintaining the culture of BeCore," Long said. "Our culture has always been Whatever It Takes, a work-hard and play-hard environment. It has been the key to our success and, most important, our happiness as a team."

To emphasize the play-hard aspect of the culture, BeCore needed to revive the connected feeling among very busy people and increasingly complex staff interactions. It's happening now, from conversations at weekly team meetings to special events. "At our end-of-summer celebration, we got to dunk our CEO and chief marketing officer in a dunk tank in exchange for all the long hours, traveling and stress our busiest season brings," Long said. "We bond on a larger scale, and we also create a welcoming and fun environment for the new members joining our family."

That end-of-summer event was a picture-perfect conversation starter brought on-site: a taco catering truck, a colorful piñata game and a dunking machine. Without any predetermined expectation, digitally savvy employees naturally pulled out their smartphones to share the visual story via Instagram with each other and their broader networks. They bonded around a shared escapade consistent with their company's mission to create fun, memorable experiences for their clients. As one employee said, "Everyone was snapping pictures and posting them to show what we were doing. I was telling my personal impressions about working at a place where I get to do cool things. I wanted people to see me in a dunk tank—I'd never done that before. We want to keep the culture of the company fun."[12] A photo conversation worked, as pictures tell a story and will keep retelling it.

Whether in large or small companies, employees need supportive links to each other, especially in times of change. Storytelling, group discussions, and the grapevine transmit emotion, humanness, and personal intensity that a handbook or a presentation cannot. Of course, formal channels still deliver strategic information—a consistent explanation for what's new and the direction of progress. The conversation, though, is what helps people truly understand an issue and see its relevance at their work level. Small companies—without a structured function or an employee communicator—already rely on conversation. Large companies can build conversations about change right into the communication plan.

⭐ Juniper Networks offers an example of communicating the direction of progress and helping people see its relevance to them as the company evolves. Juniper Networks was created in 1996 to Connect Everything, Empower Everyone. Since its founding, Juniper has grown to a US$4.4-billion global enterprise. CEO Kevin Johnson joined Juniper in 2008 with a commitment to make the company the next US$10-billion technology leader. In what might have seemed counterintuitive when the global economic downturn hit in 2008, the company invested significantly in research and development. The objective: emerge from the economic recession as an even stronger player in the marketplace.

Innovation was the cultural byword, and the vision for the next decade was called The New Network, foreseeing a future of networking that is open, scalable, simple, secure and automated. As Juniper was revealing this vision, the company would also announce a new business strategy, products and solutions, partnerships, and corporate brand identity. For The New Network to be successful, the company would need the full support and commitment of its 9,000-strong workforce—the people charged with turning this vision into reality. Therefore, it was imperative to engage and involve employees on the ground floor of this ambitious global initiative and in the launch of these important strategic announcements.

So Johnson delivered a written invitation to all employees to join in The New Network journey. He appeared by video to inspire employees to recognize how Juniper could change the world with each individual's pursuit for a better way. In quarterly meetings with employees, he explained that it's not about connecting equipment; it's about changing the world, complete with a Juniper manifesto.

But it takes even more than that. The communication team wanted to help the CEO listen and talk to employees about the things most important to him, like solving customers' problems. The avenue would

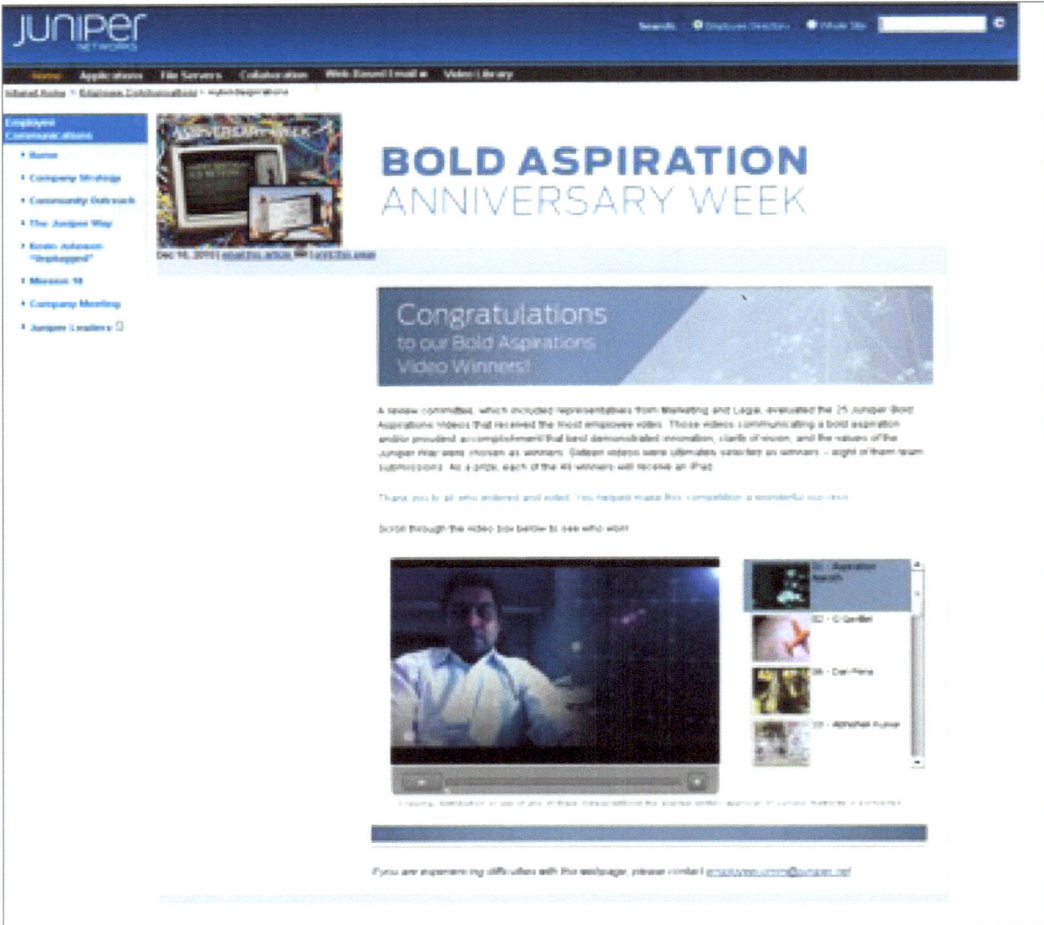

A year after the introduction of a new core value of bold aspirations at Juniper Networks, employees submitted videos to add their experiences to the conversation[14]. The screen shot is low resolution but still shows visibility the program gained on the intranet.

be intimate question-and-answer sessions with 30 to 50 employees at a time. People were asked to sign up, and they were treated to a conversation—no slides or presentation.

He wasn't there to listen to what employees were saying for the purpose of better knowing how to convince or motivate them to move the company profits higher. He listened to know how to better lead the company, to make changes in his own actions and those of his executives. Because he heard mostly about problems with scaling up the operations smoothly to accommodate Juniper's rapid growth—from having a laptop that didn't work to the inability to get computer access—an executive was hired to oversee a new scalability process.

These question-and-answer sessions, called Unplugged, also made for good video. Communicators clipped the best sound bites for "best of" videos for all employees.

In an organization the size of Juniper Networks, the CEO can't carry the communication load alone.

Senior leaders, in groups of three at a time, then met with 30 to 50 employees to talk about the company values in the business context. The meetings were branded as the Trio Tour, showing that executives were on the same page as the CEO.

WE GET IT; WE'RE CHANGING. NOW WHAT DO WE ACTUALLY NEED TO DO?

After a year of talking about culture and vision, a survey of Juniper employees confirmed that they had a high level of appreciation for the values of the company. However, the way they could apply the core value of "bold aspirations" to their own jobs was not so clearly evident to employees, at least not yet.

"Sometimes they don't connect dots from the aspiration vision and what they do day-to-day," said Stacey Clark Ohara, employee communication senior director.[13] She and her team conceived of a way for employees to tell their stories about Bold Aspirations and their work: a video submission contest for cash and gifts. All employees could vote for winning entries. Together, they would find shared meaning in their work within the new cultural framework.

"We wanted people to be really specific in their videos about how they were supporting the vision and culture, telling us their proudest accomplishment for 2010. Why were you proud, and how does it relate to The New Network and Empower Everyone? What are you trying to stretch yourself to do, and how does that help your company? What are you proud of and why?" she explained.

The video storytelling was fun and effective. "Some people were so creative, adding audio and graphics. They put a lot of effort into this. It was not just slapped together," Clark Ohara said. "People took so much pride in it, and that shows their commitment to their company." An "incredible level of participation" confirmed that employees viewed the video submissions as they voted on the ones that were meaningful to them.

> ### The trend of gamification
>
> Gamification refers to applying game elements in a way that can improve communication. Through game design techniques and psychology, gamification seeks to engage people in a way that leads to envisioning progress, accepting challenge, mastering skills and adopting desired behaviors. People interactively achieve something together for fun and rewards while solving common problems. Yes, fun. Work is what you have to do. Play is what you want to do. With gamification, work and play come together.

Perhaps even better, she said, is that it made the world a smaller place: "You got to hear the point of view from folks in India, Europe and the U.S. To hear what an engineer in India is most proud of transcends geography. It brings to life the vision of the company." The Juniper communication team immediately began planning a second video submission program.

As Juniper Networks found, employees will help communicate on a topic when they have guidance about how to do it. Supporters got a voice. Fence sitters and detractors heard them. We all talk around the water cooler, even if the water cooler has gone online.

Workplace conversations are as common as a piece of furniture at your company:

- Simply by chatting—or what we might call the grapevine, gossip or the rumor mill—employees come to a shared understanding of their work.

- Gossip pops from a kernel of truth and spreads because it makes sense to the community. Listen for the points that are exaggerated; they are what the community considers important. Recognize which points are ignored, a signal they are considered irrelevant or unclear. You can then respond to reduce confusion and improve understanding.

- When employees in a community put their ideas about work into words—or images—during a conversation, they solidify their thoughts about culture and goals. It is an always-evolving dialogue, because our working lives are constantly progressing.

- As the grapevine moves online, employee communication directors have a chance not only to listen but also to encourage more conversation. A formal communication plan can give voice to supporters, clarify misunderstandings among detractors and engage fence sitters.

Notes

1   A. Filip, personal communication, 2003.

2   M. Ward, personal communication, 2011.

3   Newell, E. (2012, February 15). *Making young employees feel at home*. Retrieved from http://www.govexec.com/management/management-matters/2012/02/going-native/41206/

4   Gladwell, M. (2002). *The tipping point: How little things can make a big difference*. Boston: Little, Brown and Company.

5   Dunbar, R. (1993). Co-evolution of neocortex size, group size, and language in humans. *Behavior and Brain Sciences*, 16(6), 681–735.

6   RPI: News & Events - Minority Rules: Scientists Discover Tipping Point for the Spread of Ideas. (2011, July 25). *Rensselaer Polytechnic Institute News & Events*. Retrieved from http://news.rpi.edu/update.do?artcenterkey=2902&setappvar=page%281%29
     Xie, J., Sreenivasan, S., Korniss, G., Zhang, W., Lim, C., & Szymanski, B. K. (2011). Social consensus through the influence of committed minorities. *Physical Review E, 84*(1).

7   RedBalloon. (2010). 45% of workers plan to leave their employer within 12 months. [*press release*], para. 19. Retrieved from http://prwire.com.au/pr/25074/45-of-workers-plan-to-leave-their-employer-within-12-months

8   Crampton, S., Hodge, J. W., & Mishra, J. M. (1998, Winter). The informal communication network: Factors influencing grapevine activity. *Public Personnel Management,* 27, 569–584.

9   Crampton, Hodge & Mishra.

10   Mishra, J. M. (1990). Managing the grapevine. *Public Personnel Management,* 19(2), 213–229.

11   W. Long, personal communication, 2012.

12   Anonymous employee, personal communication, 2012.

13   S. Clark Ohara, personal communication, 2011–2012.

14   Juniper Networks. Bold Aspiration anniversary week. Retrieved from Juniper Networks intranet.

CHAPTER 11: GO TO THE EDGE

Social media present a virtual world of opportunities to increase the strengths of small-, mid-sized- and large-company communication. They provide CEOs with another way to interact with employees, enable management to wire communication into operational processes and team activities that are increasingly happening online, and help conversations to flourish as communities thrive in social networks.

I would rather refer to these new tools and networks within the employee communication realm as *conversation media* to encourage their use for two-way, balanced, excellent communication. Other people have adopted the term *social business*, describing the collaboration that social media allow to help employees connect with dispersed teams or tap experts to accomplish the job.

YOUR ASSIGNMENT IS CHANGING, AGAIN

Since the employee communication strength of large companies is in media, and that of small companies is in conversation, conversation media are a natural fit for companies of any size. The truth is, your employees are already connecting via social media, whether as Gladwell's manageable size of 150 people who share interests or Dunbar's dozen in a support group.

How might you be there, too, listening to pinpoint what employees don't understand? How can you assist in their quest for meaning and influence their discussion to lead to shared understanding?

Shel Holtz, of Holtz Communications + Technology, makes three distinct points about social media that together explain how the employee communication discipline is broadening:

- Social business is the digital conversation we have in the day-to-day conduct of what we do.
- Word of mouth jumps digital clusters (or communities, or tribes) to create buzz.
- People are increasingly going out to the edges—to their social media networks—to get information instead of from traditional media.

"We have to be prepared, if we're going to have our messages be understood, to participate in the kinds of activities that get our messages placed out on the edge, where the attention of the audience has shifted," Holtz said.[1] The "new" employee communication becomes more conversational, moving to the edge in online communities. Social media are integrated into operational routines, part of employees' day-to-day business.

> The "new" employee communication becomes more conversational, moving to the edge in online communities. Social media are integrated into operational routines, part of employees' day-to-day business.

Even though conversation media might still feel awkwardly edgy, remember this is still media—something you know well. Business executives are becoming more comfortable with it, too.

As employee communication directors become more proficient at embedding conversation points in peer dialogue, social media will play a prominent role in moving employees toward understanding strategic goals and culture. You have another means for instigating discussion on a timely topic or pending project in a way that unites people, just as they might talk among themselves after reading a magazine article or attending a town hall meeting.

In blending conversation media into your established media mix, you also send a cultural message to employees: They are important as your company advances technologically, because they are part of the collaborative and interactive evolution.

There are many ways you can enlist opinion leaders to talk online about how individuals can succeed in their changing jobs. You can sow the kernels of conversation, listen, and then refine messages or adjust direction. Give supporters consistent knowledge about a topic, clarify topics for detractors, and help people reach shared understanding, augmenting face-to-face conversation—all the puzzle pieces to put together a communication picture for your enterprise.

The tipping point is upon us. After years of doing traditional media internally, CEOs and their employee communication directors are learning to bring new methods to their familiar workplace. "We've been trained for mass media. We have to move from producing carefully crafted messages for distribution to methods that allow us to get high levels of engagement from employees," Holtz advised.

TELL THE STORY

One way to move the conversation to the edge and engage employees is with a blog. Good blogs tell stories that engage people not only to comment on the blog site, but also to continue the conversation with peers.

⭐ Tim Hockey, CEO of TD Canada Trust, and the 30,000 employees he leads, tell stories about customer service on an employee blog to reinforce the company culture. "We have tens of thousands of these stories, and we celebrate the winners of the best stories each year," Hockey told the *Financial Post*.[2] One of his favorites is from a group of bank branch employees who wondered about a customer who usually came in daily but hadn't been there for three days. They called a social services agency that broke down the door and found the customer trapped under a chest of drawers. "If they hadn't cared enough to make that call, that customer likely would have died," Hockey said.[3]

Stories like this one reflect a deep culture of caring. When one community of employees shares a story like this one, and then someone posts it online, it jumps digital clusters to faraway employees who would not have heard the story. In one anecdote after another, peers are influencing each other's behaviors.

Caring behavior ripples into customer satisfaction...and then to each TD Canada employee's paycheck, connecting the dots from his or her particular job to corporate goals through culture. Hockey explained that "every single employee in the bank, including myself... has a portion of our compensation tied to our customer satisfaction ratings and index. That's a hard way of wiring the culture."[4]

COMFORTABLE CONVERSATION CAN TURN UNCOMFORTABLE

Conversation media are not always for sharing feel-good stories, of course. Excellent communication leaves open the possibility of messy exchanges and even conflict. Hockey is appreciative that TD Canada Trust employees feel comfortable enough to be open and honest in their conversations. "When

> **Remember:**
> Excellent communication requires dialogue, recognizing that managing conflict and confusion is a step toward shared meaning.

we make decisions that aren't great decisions, our employees tell us. I remember I made one decision once that was so bad I reversed it the next day, and on our employee blog, I wrote a post titled, 'What was I thinking?' In it, I essentially said good on you for calling me on a bad decision and we'll make it right."[5]

Taking the time to listen and appreciating a different view enough to modify your opinion is what distinguishes excellent communication with employees. "They want to know why and have a voice," Hockey affirmed.[6]

Not all CEOs or employee communication directors are comfortable with tough conversations online. But these conversations are happening anyway because social media are the *new* way that communication happens in a workplace. People float ideas, ask questions, define value and find commonality—online.

> ### Social media are the new way that communication happens in a workplace. People float ideas, ask questions, define value and find commonality—online.

"A lot of leaders are too eager to get to consensus without first hearing dissenting viewpoints. You've got to get through dissent before you get to consensus. This is particularly true when you're the CEO," said David Sacks, CEO of Yammer.[7] Another tool that gives employees a voice, Yammer is a Twitter-like social network designed for people inside companies.

⭐ Sacks told the story of an unpopular policy change at Deloitte Australia. Within a week, 168 people were discussing it on the company's Yammer network, and most didn't like it. The CEO identified the person with the most passionate views and had coffee with him. The policy was changed the next day.

It's not so much about changing people's minds as it is reaching a shared understanding. In this case, it could as easily have gone the other way, with the dissenter getting clarification and becoming a supporter.

Consider these 168 commenters as a tribe around a campfire. This campfire is the social object—a topic of discussion in this case—that people had an interest in and gathered around to discuss. They asked questions like:

- What's causing this?
- Is there news someone can share?
- What can you show me?
- What does everyone else think about this?
- Are we supposed to do something about it?

On Facebook, the campfire could be family photos that bring people together. With Foursquare, the social object may be a location people like to visit.

Employee communicators can initiate a social object and start a conversation. Other times, they depend on influencers already around a campfire discussion. When the tribe gathers, people listen to the chief, just as employees look to their leader and appreciate the support they give just by listening.

In the story Sacks told, that particular conversation happened as it ideally would in small companies, as CEOs explain the executive vision and expectation, and employees listen in order to make informed suggestions. They each contribute to solving problems and making decisions in a way that leads to a shared understanding.

WE'RE ALL STILL LEARNING

The difference is in the tools—the conversation media—that we have now. You may be one of the people who tweets from your smartphone on the way to meet with a client, asking someone from your digital community of colleagues to recommend a good restaurant nearby for lunch, and, in the process, ending up at a Pinterest collection of photos of entrees. But not everyone is attracted to new technology or thinks it adds value for them. Looking up a restaurant review from the desktop computer before leaving for lunch works just fine. Those may be the people who will see the learning curve for social media as a steep hill. You will need an adoption plan along with your communication plan for CEOs, managers, and other employees.

Moving to the edge today doesn't require moving outside the comfort of a secure company network, if that is a concern. You can use your enterprise platform, as internal networks replicate social media capabilities that consumers use on the Internet. You can hold a video chat; use internal instant messaging; or build a wiki with a collaboration tool.

And like the consumer world, employee communication is going mobile as workers increasingly look for information on their smartphones and tablets. Social business makes processes and tasks more mobile, with options for text, graphics, audio and video. Employees trade ideas, get answers, discuss options, come to conclusions, and make plans, wherever they are and wherever they go. Communication is wired in. Even when they are not face to face, people appreciate getting help solving problems, and they like to feel like they are helping others. Teams take their on-the-job supportive relationships and reminders of how their work furthers business goals with them. They do their jobs better, together, even virtually.

Soon, we will have more advanced tools that delineate a new, even further out, edge on which we place a social object for a tribe to gather around and discuss. The goal for us remains the same: two-way communication among employees in communities to clarify and improve understanding. The patterns for excellent communication are in place for us to use, whatever lies ahead.

Reflections on putting symmetrical conversation into social media:

- Social media combine the strength of large-business communication in mass media with the strength of CEO conversation in small companies and wired-in communication in medium-sized companies—for *conversation media*.

- Social media allow employee communication directors and CEOs to meet people where they are, on the edge, conversing in their communities.

- Social media amplify communication, as listeners on the edge of a community move the message out to other communities.

- As different or confusing as each new social media tool may seem, consider how conversation media improve the way you communicate so that your company thrives. Turn consistent messages into personally relevant conversations.

Notes

1 S. Holtz, personal communication, 2012.

   For ongoing insight into communication and technology, subscribe to the For Immediate Release podcast. http://www.firpodcastnetwork.com

2 Bitti, M. T. (2011, August 30). Bank where people make the difference. *Financial Post*, para. 5. Retrieved from http://business.financialpost.com/executive/bank-where-people-make-the-difference?__lsa=29f4-c673

3 Bitti, para. 5.

4 Bitti, para. 7.

5 Bitti, para. 7.

6 Bitti, para. 7.

7 Ludwig, A. (2011, September 12). Making Dilbert obsolete—Yammer's CEO on software for corporate transformation. *Forbes*, para. 22. Retrieved from http://www.forbes.com/sites/techonomy/2011/09/19/david-sacks-on-how-his-company-is-harnessing-social-power/

CHAPTER 12: PUT IT INTO PRACTICE

Feeling a little overwhelmed? You might be, unless you are one of the lucky ones already working in a company where most employees feel supported and surrounded by solid values, and where people usually understand how their jobs relate to goals that are firmly based in the organization's culture. Keep doing more of the same.

Otherwise, where do you start when looking for the right topic and venue for a CEO to communicate with employees? How do you go about integrating communication into operations or using media for the right reasons?

If you are convinced you should try new patterns, take it one step at a time. One project, one department, as if it were a small company.

We've learned here that excellent management is the breeding ground for excellent communication. Regrettably, not everyone works in a company with consistently excellent management, but almost every company has pockets of excellence. Find one of those and creatively rearrange your communication puzzle pieces:

- Partner with a manager who recognizes shortcomings in certain operations and thinks better communication could help.

- Respond to a request to write or publish a message by proposing a different approach, one that capitalizes on an opportunity from a different-sized company.

- Identify a communication topic in need of shared understanding among employees to make a powerful difference.

Keep your eye on the strengths list as you go.

Employee communication strength
CEO as communicator through conversation about business goals and culture
Communication of goals and culture integrated within business operations and processes
Consistent messages through internal "mass" media to improve understanding of strategic goals and culture

When this chart appeared in Chapter 3, it had a company size linked to each strength, since these approaches happen traditionally and more naturally in companies of a particular size. No longer—now you can claim them all.

You can put excellent communication into practice in just three steps.

1. INTENTIONAL PURPOSE

First, pick the topic or project to which you will intentionally apply a newly discovered strength from outside your traditional arsenal or one you perhaps already have mastered. A good topic or project to start with is one whose message has the potential to:

- Establish supportive relationships on the job.
- Provide information about how employees' work fits in with and furthers business goals.
- Do both of the above.

This simple planning exercise will get you started in deciding how to present a topic so it has meaning employees can share. Write down your ideas in each of these boxes.

Here's how my communication topic or initiative will...

...establish supportive relationships on the job:

...help employees understand how their work fits into current and future business goals:

2. INTENTIONAL DELIVERY

Next, decide how you can use your strengths to deliver that message and how you can try opportunities you might not have considered before, because you thought they were too far outside your box.

With intentional delivery, you decide how to send a uniting message for that particular topic in an excellent way. It doesn't have to be your current, expected path.

Here's how, in voicing the uniting message about this topic or project, our...

...*CEO* can reinforce our business goals and culture:

...managers can explain the connection between larger issues and specific job matters within *operations*:

...internal *media* can reinforce and ensure consistency:

3. INTENTIONAL CONVERSATION

Conversations—particularly the personal examples embedded in them—help people know that others think and feel like they do. Stories make a connection that is first emotional, then logical.

As you build in conversation options, be open to the likelihood that your communication plan may need to be refined based on what's being said along the way as you listen to your community or audience. You may even hear a reason to suggest that your executives modify the decision or action being communicated.

Here's how...

…I can listen to supervisors and help them understand this topic and get comfortable talking with employees about it:

…I can enlist opinion leaders on this topic, listen to their thoughts and explain it to other employees:

…I can listen to the grapevine, give supporters information about this topic and improve understanding among detractors:

By taking the time to write down your thoughts on these three steps, you will see your employee communication effort more sharply and more conspicuously as part of the excellent management of your company. You will identify how to model symmetrical communication for understanding, not persuasion.

These *Give Voice To What Unites Us* boxes you've filled in with intentional purpose, intentional delivery and intentional conversation present patterns to expand on within your traditional communication plan. It's pre-work, a thinking process that helps you step outside your box. You now have insight for creating your roadmap for implementation using your regular communication planning process.[1] Your prefilled boxes will guide you in writing the statement of situation or opportunity, identifying your target community or audience, setting communication objectives that address business goals, creating messages and implementing a solution, and finally measuring or evaluating your success—the elements of a tried-and-true communication work plan.

First, do your Give Voice to What Unites Us pre-work   **Then, create a standard communication work plan**

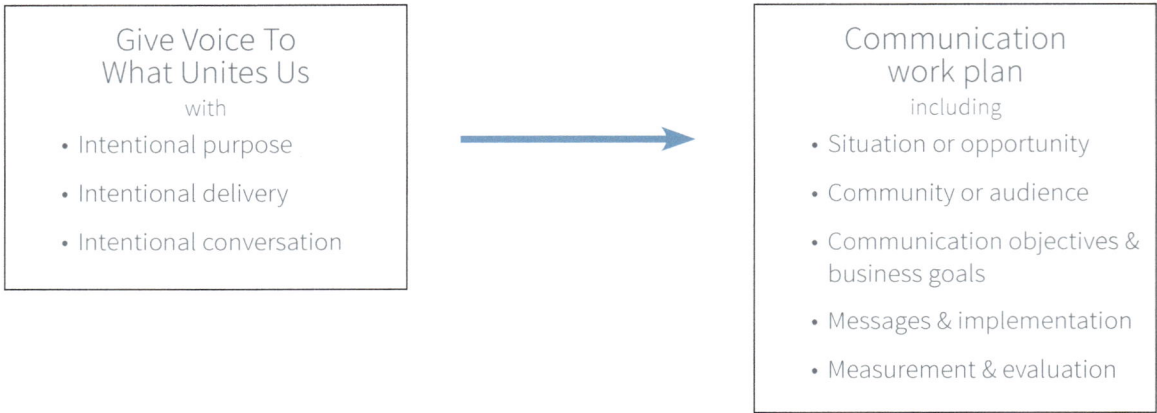

Give Voice To What Unites Us with		Communication work plan including
• Intentional purpose	→	• Situation or opportunity
• Intentional delivery		• Community or audience
• Intentional conversation		• Communication objectives & business goals
		• Messages & implementation
		• Measurement & evaluation

Think first about giving voice to what unites us––intentional purpose, intentional delivery and intentional conversation––for an informed perspective on developing your communication plan

This pre-work does not give you a so-called best practices campaign to mimic. Instead, you will see how the patterns of excellent communication actually fit your unique company vision and culture. You can assemble puzzle pieces to keep you centered on creating an excellent communication plan. "Be a yardstick of quality," Apple's co-founder Steve Jobs said. "Some people aren't used to an environment where excellence is expected." So set your expectations, fully understand what you can accomplish, know what it takes and include all the people in your organization.

Be an excellent communicator, starting today.

Notes

1   For general information about how to develop an employee communication plan after your *Give Voice To What Unites Us* pattern analysis for intentional purpose, delivery and conversation:

https://www.iabc.com/the-strategic-communication-plan/

http://www.ragan.com/Main/Articles/How_to_write_an_internal_communication_strategy_48293.aspx

To continue the conversation about excellent employee communication, visit the Employee Communication Excellence Community on Google+.

INDEX

GIVE VOICE TO WHAT UNITES US

GIVE VOICE TO WHAT UNITES US

Thinking Big, Staying Small, 19, 23-24

Time magazine, 13

Tindell, K., 28

Transformational leadership, 55

Tribes, 63, 66, 73, 75-76

Trident Precision Manufacturing Inc., 29

Trust through communication, 47, 55, 66-67

Twitter, 38-39, 75-76

Two-way communication, 10-11, 19-20, 25, 29-30, 32-33, 38-40, 42, 46-47, 49-50, 54, 57-58, 61, 73, 76. *See also* Symmetrical communication

U

Undercover boss, 13

Unite, unify, 9, 21, 40, 46, 68, 74, 80, 82

U.S. Consumer Product Safety Commission, 64

U.S. Steel, 32

V

Values, 20-21, 24, 26, 28-30, 33, 35, 42, 44, 46-47, 58, 61, 68, 71, 78

Video, 12-13, 24, 32, 37, 39, 45, 47, 53, 58, 69-71, 76

Vision, company, 17, 20-21, 23-25, 32-33, 37, 42-46, 52, 69, 71, 75, 82

Vitiello Communications Group, 24. *See* VTLO

Vitiello, J., 24-25

Voice, employee, 40, 43-44, 46, 66, 71-72, 75, 82

VTLO, 24-25

W

Ward, M., 58, 61-62, 64, 66

Watson, T., 9-10, 35

Web conferencing, 39

Wellspring, 52, 61

Wendover, R., 64

Whatever It Takes, 68

Williams, R., 55

Wired-in communication, 20-21, 26, 28-33, 44, 50, 73, 76

Word of mouth, 73. *See* Peer to peer communication

Work furthers business goals, 8, 10, 13, 16, 18, 23-25, 28-29, 31-33, 36-40, 43-59, 63-65, 67-68, 70-72, 76, 79, 82

Workwise Communication, 47

Y

Yammer, 39, 75

YouTube, 38

www.ingramcontent.com/pod-product-compliance
Lightning Source LLC
Chambersburg PA
CBHW042049210326
41519CB00052B/186